To Ruth —
    with appreciation for your part
in my thinking, (tho unacknowledged
in this book) — and with my
affection —
                    Helen

May 1957.

ESSENTIALS OF SOCIAL GROUP WORK SKILL

ESSENTIALS OF SOCIAL GROUP WORK SKILL

_____ Helen U. Phillips

ASSOCIATION PRESS—NEW YORK

To

KENNETH L. M. PRAY

whose varied and profound contribution
to the social work profession and to the author
is our valued heritage

Preface

THE REQUIREMENT AND WRITING of a doctoral dissertation presented me with the opportunity to explore the definition and use of social group work skill in its relation to purpose, and to organize my study of it in written form. While this volume is addressed primarily to social group work practitioners, educators, and students, it is my hope that it will be provocative and useful to others who work with groups as a means of moving toward the purposes of the groups and of their sponsoring institutions, such as churches, schools, and casework agencies. For it is my opinion that social group work is a method that can be used in any institutional setting where social purposes are held.

I have endeavored to present only one theoretical base for the way in which people can be helped to use group experience to the enrichment of themselves and society. Although there are various psychological and theoretical bases for social group work practice, I have been gratified to observe that two or more "camps" of group workers have not developed over the past decade. Credit for this state of affairs is due, I believe, to the deliberate efforts of a number of group workers and group work educators. Readers will find that, in many respects, much of what I have written is compatible with some views presented in other recent group work literature, the content of which has contributed to my thinking. Some undeniable differences will be found, however, notably in the chapters on the use of agency function and the use of the present. It is hoped that the reader will choose to cover Part I before turning to Part II.

Assuredly, I make no claim that the functional way of helping described in the following pages is the only way, or even the ideal way of working with groups toward social goals. It is the method in which I have conviction and which I know to be effective in practice from the tested experience of the students whom I have taught.

It is my hope that this volume, rather than tending to divide our relatively young specialization of the social work profession, may contribute to furthering the united purpose of social group workers and to the improvement of social group work skill.

*   *   *

To name all of the people who have contributed—some of them unwittingly—to the development of the ideas expressed in the pages that follow is neither possible nor appropriate. I have received clarity and direction, question and challenge, in varying degrees, from my faculty colleagues, former and present, in the University of Pennsylvania School of Social Work; from supervisors in the School's field-training agencies; and from the students whom it has been my privilege to teach.

I am indebted to the group work agency executives who permitted me to use their agency records in this publication.

                                                H.U.P.

Contents

Introduction

IN ALL FORMS OF LIFE, group associations are operating, so that it may be said that the interdependence of parts to comprise a functioning whole is a universal phenomenon. It is not fortuitous that the people and governments of the world are presently engaged, through "summit" conferences, in seeking ways to co-operate with each other. They are impelled to such engagement by the dawning recognition of co-operative relationships as essential to the progress of human society and, indeed, to existence itself, and hence are searching for new and appropriate forms to facilitate positive interaction.

But one is not limited to contemplation of the vastness of contemporary human society for illumination on the universal quality of the interdependence of constituent parts for wholeness. From a steady accumulation of scientific studies in several disciplines, there is abundant evidence that in all stages of all forms of life are patterns of necessary relations between parts that comprise a whole, if the parts are to thrive and grow.

Illustrative of such studies is Allee's work on the social life of animals, in which he concludes that the natural impulses of animals compel them, if they are to live, to co-operate with like forms of life in unique structures that require varying degrees of organization. "Evidently mutual interdependence, or automatic co-operation is sufficiently widespread among the animal kingdom to warrant the conclusion . . . that it ranks as one of the fundamental qualities of animal protoplasm and probably of protoplasm in general." [1]

From biology comes the conclusion that interdependence starts at the point of origin of new life forms. For example, in a recent volume, carefully documented by sources from both the natural and social sciences, Ashley-Montagu develops the idea that the pattern of social relationships is a natural continuation of the processes of biological growth. ". . . the source of the social appetite of all living creatures is traceable to the way in which the living organism originates. All cells originate from other cells; it is impossible for them to originate in any other way. . . . Each cell of the organism is dependent for its proper functioning upon the interaction with it of every other cell of the organism. Which is to say that every organism functions as a whole, and not as a mass of discrete, independent cellular elements. The organism is itself a dependent and interdependent whole." [2] Montagu thus invests the social appetite of man with an instinctive qual-

ity, derived from the biological growth process and consistent with it.[3]

The same concept of the existence of mutuality has
found expression in quite another field—theology. A contemporary theological scholar, Cherbonnier, writing of
the corporate character of human existence, says: "Spir-
itually, morally and emotionally speaking, there is no
such thing as an isolated individual. As the Bible puts it,
'We are members one of another' (Romans 12:5; Ephesians
4:25), not in any merely metaphorical sense, but at the
most real and decisive level." [4]

Proceeding on the premise that interdependence is universal and that, to some extent, it is a natural part of the
process of life, we come to the question of the value of
co-operation in our culture, and the connection between
the value placed on it and the kind of training developed
to further it. For inevitable as mutual dependence may be,
the forms that carry and facilitate it are developed to their
maximum usefulness to society through training that supplements its natural presence.[5]

That group associations are valued highly in our culture is implicit in the incidence of groups in our society
and in the amount of attention that is given to establishing and developing them. High value is placed, in our
contemporary American society, on the ability to get
along with one's fellow men, not only with the family
group and those with like interests and experiences, but
with those with sharp differences. One of the criteria for
judging individual development is the degree of social
adaptation manifested. In such diverse areas as education,

politics, religion, economics, people participate in groups to pursue their interests and to deepen social values. One of the results of engagement with others in groups is learning—the acquisition of ideas and skills and whatever the experience provides of benefit to one's self in relation to others.

Groups lend themselves to training experiences. Indeed, one might say that one of the functions of groups is to train toward whatever the defined purpose of the group may be. The continuous development of formal education through groups, in contrast to the earlier tutorial system, is illustrative of the value given to groups as a channel for learning.[6] The extensive studies made by social anthropologists of the nature and use of groups in widely varied cultures reveal the numerous group patterns which have been developed around both play and work, to train children in the fundamentals of their culture, which include co-operative living.[7]

Adler points to both the value of co-operation and the necessity of preparing or training for it: "The individual's proper development can only progress if he lives and strives as a part of the whole. The shallow objection of individual systems has no meaning as against this view. . . . All our bodily and mental functions are rightly, normally and healthily developed insofar as they are imbued with sufficient social feeling and are fitted for co-operation. . . . All the problems of human life demand capacity for co-operation and preparation for it—the visible sign of social feeling." [8]

Even with such slight evidence as afforded by these few

illustrations from a limited number of fields and studies, it is clear that both the need and value of group associations are universal to man. Social group work, the subject of this volume, far from inventing and imposing a foreign or untested set of values, has developed on the foundation of this universal need for group associations and on the base of the accepted value given to such associations in our culture. It has developed its unique forms and methods for meeting this common need and for perpetuating its values. People of the communities where group work agencies offer their services demand groups. Group workers respond to these demands by providing opportunities for participation in groups as a means of individual development through increased socialization and co-operative living. If they are to contribute to the fulfillment of such goals, they must possess a reliable skill, and we turn our attention next to the meaning of professional skill.

THE NATURE OF SKILL

Possession of a skill that can be communicated is one of the marks of a profession. To the social workers gathered together at a national meeting forty years ago, it must have been both encouraging and challenging to have their various activities considered and tested against the criteria of a profession as stated by a distinguished member of an already established profession. One of the six criteria of true professions, said Dr. Abraham Flexner, is that "they possess a technique capable of communication through a highly specialized educational discipline." [9] Now, forty years later, social work is increasingly recognized as a

profession, and the skills essential to professional performance in social work, although in a continuous state of
being tested and refined, can be communicated.

The subject of this writing is the skill essential to one
of the specializations of social work; [10] namely, social
group work. There is growing conviction among social
work practitioners and educators that there is a process
generic to all of social work, but that each specialization
also has characteristics of process unique to it. Thus one
group work educator writes: "There is a core of knowledge and skill generic to all social work practice but there
are also some specifics, theoretical and pragmatic, essential
to developing insights and skill in any one of the major
processes in social work." [11] This study is concerned with
selected aspects of social group work skill, some of which
are unique to it and some held in common with other social work specializations.

In a general sense, skill means the capacity to perform.
The Webster dictionary defines it as "knowledge of, and
expertness in, execution and performance." An intriguing
and now archaic definition of skill as an intransitive verb
is: "to make a difference." This same essence of change
is conveyed by the definition of skill to which Virginia
Robinson refers as "the capacity to set in motion and control a process of change in specific material in such a way
that the change that takes place in the material is effected
with the greatest degree of consideration for and utilization of the quality and capacity of the material." [12]

The skill conceptualized by such definitions derives
from both the knowledge and the experience through

practice of the person who possesses it. If the social group worker is to be helpful to the persons he serves, he must know and understand the basic sociological and psychological concepts of human growth through relationships, use these concepts in relating sensitively to the members of his groups "with the greatest degree of consideration for the quality and capacity of the material," [13] and actively and consciously initiate and control a process with his groups "utilizing the quality and capacity of the material." [14]

The components of knowing, feeling, and acting are in this conception of skill, and therefore this inquiry, in part, will be directed to examining the values and contributive theory that underlie group work skill, as well as the method by which these values and theories may be translated into practice for the help of those whom the group worker serves.

Method, by dictionary definition, is "an orderly procedure or process." Trecker, a group work educator, defines it in a recently published volume as follows: "A method is a conscious procedure, a designed means of achieving a goal. In its outer aspects, a method is a way of doing something, but underneath the doing we always discover an integrated arrangement of knowledge, understanding and principles." [15] He goes on to distinguish between method and skill: "Method means the purposeful use of insights and understandings based upon a body of knowledge and principles. Skill is the capacity to apply knowledge and understanding to a given situation." [16] Method is use of a process; skill is capacity to use it. Although both method and skill will be presented in this study by the introduction and analysis of a number of records of the process between group worker and group in single group meetings, our central interest is in the skill essential to the worker's effective use of group work method.[17]

But group work skill, method, theories, and values are not developed without central direction, and that direction stems from the basic group work purpose. To conceive of purpose as the focus for developmental process is by no means the unique discovery of the social group worker. Sinnott, an eminent biologist, ascribes the process of plant and animal growth to the "purpose" of the protoplasm, and defines that purpose as the development of an organism. "Life has its physical base in that remarkable material system which is called *protoplasm*. . . . The task of the biologist is therefore to understand this remarkable living material. From it are built the beautiful and intricate bodies of plants and animals; in it centers the control which regulates the activities of these exquisite mechanisms; and out of it come the alterations which make possible all evolutionary change." [18] Biological growth thus conceived suggests central purpose as determining the focus from which form and organization emanate to facilitate the process of relationships. The purpose is part of the process.

Applying to social group work this concept of purpose as determining form and process, the group worker finds, in the purpose of his profession, direction for his efforts and the determinant for his selection of methods and of values to be sustained or, in brief, the determinant of the nature and application of his skill.

Scope of This Volume

Proceeding on the assumption that there is a reciprocal relation between articulated, accepted group work purpose and social group work skill, the objective of this volume is to define and elaborate on that relationship by exploring a central question: In what way does the use of specific aspects of social group work skill contribute to the fulfillment of group work purpose?

Pursuit of answers to this question leads us first, in Part One, to a study of the roots of group work skill, its purpose and philosophy, proceeding in Part Two, the major part of this writing, to consideration of the use of selected aspects of skill as they contribute to the fulfillment of purpose. From the several important areas of group work skill, four have been selected, namely, skill in using situational limitations, specifically the agency function; in communicating on a feeling level; in meeting and using the reality of the present in time; and, finally, in developing and using the relations between members.[19] By focusing on these specific and selected aspects of group work skill, it is possible to define, illustrate, and examine skill in its relation to the purpose for which it is used.

To assess the nature of skill employed to achieve ends, it is essential to know the general and precise purposes to which the skill is directed. We proceed first, therefore, to an examination of the historical development of social group work purpose as it has culminated in the present-day conception of it.

CHAPTER NOTES

1. Warder C. Allee, *Animal Aggregations* (Chicago: University of Chicago Press, 1931), p. 357. See also *The Social Life of Animals* (New York: Norton, 1938).

2. M. F. Ashley-Montagu, *On Being Human* (New York: Henry Schuman, 1950), p. 30 (reprinted by permission of the publishers Abelard-Schuman, Ltd.). Later expanded into *The Directions of Human Development* (New York: Harper, 1955).

3. Cf. Clyde Kluckhohn, Henry A. Murray, and David M. Schneider, *Personality, Society and Culture* (New York: Knopf, 1953), 2nd ed., p. 64, "The fact that human beings are mammals and reproduce bi-sexually creates a basic pre-disposition toward at least the rudiments of social living."

4. E. LaB. Cherbonnier, *Hardness of Heart* (Garden City, N. Y.: Doubleday, 1955), p. 126.

5. Ralph Linton, denying the instinctive nature of co-operation in man, calls for training for it: "Since humans lack such instincts [toward co-operation for survival], it becomes necessary to subject them to an extraordinarily long and elaborate training if they are to function successfully as members of a society." *The Tree of Culture* (New York: Knopf, 1955). Quoted in the *New York Times* Book Review, October 23, 1955.

6. Ruth Cunningham and Associates, *Understanding Group Behavior of Boys and Girls* (New York: Teachers College, Columbia University, 1951).

7. For example, Margaret Mead and Martha Wolfenstein, *Childhood in Contemporary Cultures* (Chicago: University of Chicago Press, 1955).

8. Alfred Adler, *Social Interest: a Challenge to Mankind* (London: Faber & Faber, 1938; New York: Putnam, 1938), pp. 283–284. Reprinted by permission of author's agents, Pearn, Pollinger & Higham, Ltd., London.

9. Abraham Flexner, "Is Social Work a Profession?" *Proceedings of the National Conference of Charities and Corrections,* XLII, 1915, p. 580.

10. A report of the Committee on Specializations in Social Work Education, of the Council on Social Work Education, was pre-

sented at the National Conference of Social Work, 1956, by Ruth E. Smalley in the form of a paper entitled "Specialization in Social Work Education: a Committee Report and some of its Implications for the Profession." The report includes the following statement: "Specialization in social work is conceived as process: the primary processes in direct service are social casework and social group work. Other processes are community organization, administration, supervision, consultation, teaching, and research."

11. Clara A. Kaiser, "Group Work Education in the Last Decade," *The Group,* XV, June, 1953, p. 5.

12. Virginia P. Robinson, "The Meaning of Skill," *Training for Skill in Social Casework* (Philadelphia: University of Pennsylvania Press, 1942), pp. 11–12.

13. *Ibid.*

14. *Ibid.*

15. Harleigh B. Trecker, *Social Group Work Principles and Practices,* 2nd ed. (New York: Whiteside, 1955), p. 3.

16. *Ibid.*

17. Group work literature contains descriptions, analyses, and illustrations of the social group work method: e.g., Gertrude Wilson and Gladys Ryland, *Social Group Work Practice* (Boston: Houghton Mifflin, 1949); Grace L. Coyle, *Group Work with American Youth* (New York: Harper, 1948); Trecker, *op. cit.*

18. Edmund W. Sinnott, *Cell and Psyche: the Biology of Purpose* (Chapel Hill: University of North Carolina Press, 1950), pp. 17–18.

19. Capacity to use program creatively to achieve group work goals is a notable aspect of skill that is not given separate consideration in this writing. While not frequently noted specifically in the pages that follow, it is the writer's viewpoint that the concepts of skill herein discussed apply to the worker's use of himself in introducing and developing program with his groups. For the movement toward social group work goals is consistently enhanced by the skillful use of program media.

Part **ONE**

THE ROOTS OF

SOCIAL GROUP

WORK SKILL

CHAPTER I

The Purpose of Social Group Work

BECAUSE OF THE NATURE of historical process, it can be assumed that the purpose for group work did not spring up full-blown when the term "social group work" was created [1] and conscious professionalism developed, but rather that it emerged from the historical base of the movements and agencies that had long offered services to people in groups. This manner of development would suggest that there has been some continuity of purpose over the years, although inevitably there have been modifications of central purpose, and shifts in emphasis. To identify both the continuing elements and the changes, one must turn to the "group work" literature of the past one hundred years, since for a century in the United States there have been people with enough conviction in the value of group experience to make leadership of leisure-time groups their full-time vocation, within some kind of organizational structure.[2]

It was many years before there was identification of workers of one organization with those of another with similar purposes. The early literature, therefore, even as late as the twenties, contains no discussion of general professional purpose. Available primary sources on the nature of the historical goals of group work are limited to the writings of leaders from the various organizations whose goals and work are described in terms of the specific type of agency.

THE HISTORICAL PURPOSE
OF SOCIAL SETTLEMENTS

The history of any one of the social movements that found expression in the institutional form of a social agency dealing with groups would serve as a rewarding resource for understanding group work purpose. The social settlement movement is selected for examination here because of the wealth of written material available and because it seems to have been identified relatively early with the social work profession.[3] As early as 1894, papers delivered by settlement workers made their appearance in the published proceedings of the Conference of Charities and Corrections. One settlement head-resident, while somewhat apologetic for presuming to address a group of "charity workers," identified himself and his settlement's purpose with them and their emerging purpose when he declared: ". . . the method of social elevation is not through patronage, but through mutual confidence and respect." [4]

⊢ The founders of the first social settlements in this country were motivated by the same spirit and purpose that pervaded the Englishmen who founded Toynbee Hall in London in 1884. In fact their inspiration came directly from personal visits to that original London settlement, established so that university men, imbued with the Christian ideals of social justice and humanitarianism, might live "face to face with the actual conditions of crowded city life, study on the spot their evils and remedies, and, if possible, ennoble the lives and improve the material conditions of the people.".[5] Woods and Kennedy, producing the results of a comprehensive study of settlements enhanced by many years of personal experience in the field, summarize the purpose of the early English settlements as follows:["The best product of the universities had established themselves in neglected backgrounds of London to be neighbors and fellow-citizens, there to develop skill in study and service; to reinforce the agencies of sanitation, of charity, and of education; to give fine and varied form to the pursuit of recreation; to enter into direct and sympathetic interchange with the spokesmen of industrial unrest and to take the chances of the political reformer; to seek to elicit for better things the collective and corporate initiative of the people." [6]

This, then, was the purpose that American settlement pioneers determined to attempt to fulfill, in their unique ways, as seemed appropriate to the differences in American urban and industrial communities in the nineties. In many respects, the early settlements were extensions of the individual persons who started them. The groups of "settlers" were often composed of the head-resident's friends and acquaintances who shared with him like interests and zeal for humanitarian experimentation.[7] Although each settlement was developed in a unique way, depending on its particular neighborhood and founder, all were developed with the goal of making life richer for the people of the neighborhood.

The word "neighborhood" carries traditional significance in settlement purpose. In the past sixty years every piece of literature written about settlement work, no matter what its specific topic, contains some reference to the neighborhood. Concerning the relation of the neighborhood to the purpose of the settlement, most of the writers are explicit. The most vocal and respected spokesman of the early settlement leaders, Jane Addams, speaking in 1897, said: "Perhaps the settlement aims to change the social ideals of its neighborhood more than any other one thing." [8] By way of comparison, the statement of a committee that studied the Cleveland settlements in 1946 is of interest: "The purpose which distinguishes the settlement from other groups and institutions that have the same basic philosophy, is to develop among people, in the local area it serves, a sense of neighborhood." [9] Changing the social ideals of a neighborhood and developing a sense of neighborhood are not identical goals; and yet as one reads of the kinds of contacts and activities that settlement workers, past and more recent, have precipitated to approach their goals, one knows that these two purposes are reciprocal. For the pioneers, intent on changing ideals through a variety of program that involved the neighbors, found that a new sense of neighborhood developed. And present-day workers find that a neighborhood, in the process of developing its consciousness as an entity, modifies its values.

Much of the written expression of the purpose of the pioneer settlement workers was in idealistic and, to modern readers, sentimental terms, such as "helping people to find a better way of life." But certainly there was nothing amorphous or sentimental in what these same workers accomplished! The attacks on corrupt local government, and reforms in health and industrial working conditions at the turn of the century, are part of the social history of America. It is true that much was accomplished by the personal vigor and influence of the settlement leaders as they fought for the rights of their neighbors to have more decent living. But, through group organizations and meetings, the neighbors themselves were involved in consideration and action on the problems that affected them.[10]

Throughout the development of the settlement movement there has been the steady goal of improving the social conditions of neighborhoods, and frequently of more extensive areas. Interpretation of how this goal might best be achieved has been widely varied and, indeed, it appears that in some settlements the goal has been obscured in concentration on offering exclusively recreational activities; but the social goal of neighborhood betterment has been articulated consistently. This consistency can be traced through the papers and articles of settlement leaders. A head-resident's report in 1900 presented a plea for keeping the spirit of protest for a better society and for maintaining the settlements as "hot centres of new

thought." [11] Dr. John Elliott, after twenty years of settlement experience, wrote, in 1915, of the need to develop
social conscience: "It seems to me that this should be the
real purpose of social work—not to help people just to
help themselves, but to help them to achieve a freedom
for themselves which can only be achieved through working for the freedom of others." [12] Harriet Vittum, speaking in the twenties, wondered why settlements seemed to
lose members when they reached working age, and as-
serted that "absorbing interests through practical citizenship" must be offered them.[13]

A recently published statement of settlement objectives
includes a social emphasis: "The settlement purpose is
rooted in a concern for and knowledge of neighborhoods;
the neighborhood is the 'client.' The specific objectives of
the settlement today are: (a) to help the people of the
neighborhood to live together in such a way as to become
a source of enrichment to one another in their social relationships; (b) to discover and develop indigenous leadership which will operate for the good of all people across
racial, religious, and nationality lines; and (c) to help people fulfill their citizenship responsibility to one another
and the wider community through effective patterns of
individual and group action." [14]

At the same time that settlements have held to their
basic social goal, their leaders have believed in experience
with the cultural arts as a means toward the promotion
of fuller living for the people of their neighborhoods.
Consequently, the history of the settlements is so rich
with the development of cultural activities—music, drama,

handicrafts, art, and dance—that one can conclude that a continuous purpose has been to enhance appreciation of the arts through satisfying, participating experience with them and thus to establish ever-deepening values. The director of the Settlement Music School of Philadelphia expressed this purpose in 1926 when he said, "By helping the community to see the relative importance of temporary and fundamental values, the settlement will continue to make its greatest contribution." [15]

Emphasis on the cultural arts was given impetus in the first two decades of the century by the acceleration of immigration from Europe and the resulting goal of "Americanization" of alien neighbors. Settlement leaders conceived of Americanization as a two-way process which permitted the newcomer to begin to feel part of his new country only as he contributed to it something valued from his own culture. This belief led to the encouragement of perpetuating European arts—crafts, dances, songs—in the settlement neighborhoods.[16]

There seems to have been all-pervasive educational purpose among settlements, of which the emphasis on cultural arts was only one expression. Clubs and classes, traditionally offered as part of the settlement program, centered around a variety of educational content. Some present-day settlement workers tend to interpret the educational aspect of their goals in this somewhat narrower way, with emphasis on the content to be taught. But Robert Woods, writing in 1922, interpreted the educational purpose of settlements broadly: ". . . the whole settlement programme, in all its aspects is, and must be,

educational. Let every phase of the work, for the improvement of the health, for a higher standard of living, for the
increase of happiness and joy, for ethical and spiritual
fulfillment, be conceived as educational, first and last." [17]

"The increase of happiness and joy," of which Mr.
Woods spoke in the twenties, can be recognized as the
same goal that contemporary workers express as "personality development." A curious absence of that term is
noted in the first forty years of settlement literature. But
it must me remembered that the impact of psychoanalysis
on social work thinking occurred in the twenties and that,
in the same decade, educators were becoming pupil-
centered rather than exclusively subject-centered as the
theories of "progressive education" were being developed
and tested.[18] Both of these movements had a profound influence on settlement work, as on all of group work.
While the deepest effect was upon the method for achieving goals, the influence was evident, too, in the change
in terminology and in sharper clarification of the goal of
individual development.

It was in 1931 that Miss Helen Hart, then the director
of Kingsley House in Pittsburgh, sounded a new note in
the literature in regard to the purpose of the settlement.
She spoke at a time when the economic depression of the
thirties was in its early stages and when group workers
were earnestly giving attention to methods of their work.
"In the face of standardization," said Miss Hart, "these
[settlement] houses have chosen as their central objective
the development of individual personality; and in the
face of materialism they have chosen as their tools in the

task of nonmaterial values of life, particularly the arts. . . . However, I want to suggest . . . a central objective for settlement programs—the objective of personality development through group relations." [19] This was not precisely a new idea to the settlements, since even in the nineties Julia Lathrop, describing the clubs that were part of Hull House, said: "All these clubs have a more or less serious purpose of culture; but all reach it, I suspect, chiefly through social intercourse and enjoyment." [20] But the thirties brought a clearer conception of the potentialities of "social intercourse" for personal growth and a firmer acknowledgment of it as germane to settlement purpose, which led to a new direction for the workers' efforts.

From this cursory analysis of settlement goals, it appears that the aim of social betterment has been constant, variously interpreted as meaning to change social conditions of a neighborhood and to increase the happiness of individual persons, both by personal contact with the worker and participation in cultural, educational, and social groups.

PROFESSIONAL PURPOSE OF SOCIAL GROUP WORK

Settlement purpose has been presented here as illustrative, though not necessarily typical, of the development of institutional group work purpose. Other agencies, started with a central purpose in the minds of the founders, have undergone changes in interpretation of the meaning of the purpose and its applicability to the time and place of their work. From the strands of the experience of working toward expressed goals in many separate group work agencies, a generally shared set of goals has been woven, which, as of the last two decades, might be characterized as group work purpose. A definition of common purpose has emerged from the gradual and still developing sense of professional identity among those who work with groups under a variety of auspices.

The year of 1935 is a significant date in the development of professional consciousness among group workers. In that year a separate section on Social Group Work was established as part of the National Conference of Social Work. In the same year the editors of the *Social Work Year Book* introduced the heading of "Social Group Work," listing it as one of the four major divisions of social work, and presenting a brief, unsigned article on the subject. Both of these innovations indicated a beginning acceptance of social group work as part of the social work profession, precipitated by the group workers' awareness of belonging to a helping profession. Development of group work method, and skill in using it, were well under way. The goals of the group work specialization of social work were first articulated in a definitive way in a paper presented at the 1935 National Conference of Social Work. "Group work may be defined as an educational process emphasizing the development and social adjustment of an individual through voluntary association; and the use of this association as a means of furthering socially desirable ends." [21] Both individual and social goals are explicit in this statement, reminiscent of traditional set-

tlement purpose. The emphasis that is new is conveyed
by the word "process" linked with "association."

That this was the beginning of a trend toward concentrating on process to achieve group work goals seems clear
when one reads subsequent articles, papers of the National
Conference of Social Work, textbooks, and committee reports where social group work is defined and its purpose
stated. Thus, in 1937, Grace Coyle wrote: "Social group
work aims at the development of persons through the
inter-play of personalities in group situations, and at the
creation of such group situations as provide for integrated, co-operative group action for common ends." [22]
The most comprehensive textbook yet written on group
work, published in 1949, carries the following statement
in its discussion of group work purpose: "Most social
agencies serving groups have two purposes in common:
(1) to help individuals use groups to further their development into emotionally balanced, intellectually free and
physically fit persons; (2) to help groups achieve ends desirable in an economic, political and social democracy." [23]

The American Association of Group Workers [24] has
contributed soundly to the clarification and affirmation
of professional group work goals. Since 1939, committees
have been active in identifying the unique objectives of
the group work part of professional social work. One committee, charged with drawing up a statement of the function of the group worker, produced a comprehensive and
somewhat overwhelming document which is quoted here
in part: "The objectives of the group worker include pro-
vision for personal growth according to individual capac-

ity and need, the adjustment of the individual to other persons, to groups and to society, and the motivation of the individual toward the improvement of society; the recognition by the individual of his own rights, limitations and abilities as well as the acceptance of the rights, abilities and differences of others. . . . Through experience he aims to produce those relations with other groups and the wider community which contribute to responsible citizenship, mutual understanding between cultural, religious, economic or social groupings in the community and a participation in the constant improvement of our society toward democratic goals." [25]

These selected statements, whose concepts are reiterated in most of the group work literature since 1935, reveal an undeniable continuation of the major historical goals of group work—dual in nature—individual development and social progress. The method for achieving or approaching the goals has radically changed with the years of experience and increasing attention to methodology. In fact the group work method is constantly being tested, reaffirmed, or refined as group workers' comprehension of psychological and social forces increases and as the social scene changes; but the basic purposes of helping people to develop emotionally and socially through group experience, and of helping groups to contribute to the social good, remain constant and stable.

One may ask how the two goals, inner and outer, individual and social, can be approached simultaneously. Is there conflict between focus on inner growth and the extension of one's self to the external, social area of living?

From one point of view, the answer to this question is that disrupting conflict between the two is inevitable, and that activity in relation to outside social forces so dissipates the energies that inner growth is interfered with and even blocked. There are dangers, the reasoning runs, of projecting all problems of living on the outside forces rather than finding and taking one's own responsibility.

From another viewpoint, consistency and interdependence can be found in simultaneous movement toward the dual goals, individual and social. In the group work situation, experience in part-whole relationships is unavoidable. The group member, seeking to establish his relation to the group that is the whole, can be helped by the worker to find parts of the group—the membership, program, purpose—with which he can identify, while he withholds the part of himself that does not want to be absorbed into the larger whole. In a more expansive sense, through program, the group and the individuals who comprise it become related in varying degrees, according to their readiness and interest, to the agency and community of which they are a part.

This means that in social group work is the possibility of meeting at least part of the human need to find a balance between the inner and outer forces—the individual and social—that make up the reality of life. It holds the potentiality for relating people in small encompassable parts, not only to each other but to society, as opportunities develop through programming. The development of social interests that may result in bringing about change in something outside the participants is, in group work terminology, usually called social action. A group's participation in a social program provides its members with some connection, however slight, with the forces of the outer world, helping them to explore their inner, individual relation and responsibility to it, with the exhilaration of the shared experience of group action.

Working from the philosophy that social participation contributes to individual growth, one can accept as consistent the second part of the group work purpose; namely, the development of the *group* toward socially desirable ends. To work toward this goal requires not only the worker's major concern for what is happening to each individual as he participates with the others, but conviction, too, that group action which results from a process that involves all members in thoughtful consideration of an issue, choice and decision, can contribute to the fulfillment of social goals. For in a democratic society the effectiveness of responsible action is not to be denied, and group work is committed to the development of democratic processes in its practice.

SOCIAL AGENCY PURPOSE

Up to this point we have been considering the professional purpose of social group work. But no matter how clearly the group worker comprehends the professional purpose or how fully he accepts it as direction for his efforts, he must find a way of working with the reality of another set of purposes which may be more or less inclusive, and certainly more specific; namely, the purpose of the social agency of which he is an integral part.

The term "social agency" as here used denotes that institutional structure which has been developed in our society through which services are offered to people to meet some part of their emotional or economic needs. The term "social group work agency" implies several constituent parts: the administrative board which carries part of the community expectation of the agency, the administrative or executive staff, staff-workers, and membership. The divergence among agencies is wide in respect to the degree of engagement of all constituent parts in the determination of objectives and policies. There are agencies whose boards of directors include elected representatives from the membership, or where clearly defined channels are established through which membership opinion and recommendation are registered and given consideration by administrative boards. But in current practice, by and large, agency objectives and policies are determined by the administrative board and executive staff, in whom ultimate responsibility is vested.

All group work agencies share the general professional aim of individual growth through group experience; some of them hold the objective of developing groups toward socially desirable goals. Each agency has specific purposes that have grown out of the particular community and clientele it serves, combined with the unique interests of the original and present leadership of the agency and the objectives of the national agency with which it may be affiliated. National organizations tend to express their aims in relatively broad terms, leaving the autonomous local agencies free to develop their own specific local objectives, provided that they are harmonious with the national stated purpose.

Whenever group work services are offered through agencies whose primary service is not group work (e.g., hospitals, schools, residential treatment centers), the purpose of the "host" agency or institution provides the direction for the more specific departmental goals. Whatever the specific agency purpose, it is a factor to be acknowledged and accepted, along with the general professional purpose, as a determinant of the direction for the worker's professional efforts.

THE GROUP'S PURPOSE

Every group, too, has its purpose for organizing and existing. It is consistent with the basic purpose of the profession and agency—the creative development of individuals through participation in groups—that the purpose of the group for itself must be taken into account. Indeed, implicit in the goal of group work as defined in the foregoing pages is the requirement to involve the group members in the determination of the purposes that will affect their group life. For the group worker's commitment is to democratic process, and the professional goal is of the nature that is valid and can be achieved only as the group's purpose for itself is given consideration.

The term "group purpose" is used here to indicate what the group as a whole considers to be its chief aim for being together and for pursuing certain activities and interests as a group—what they hope to accomplish. Some groups—friendship, action, or interest groups—may ap-

proach an agency with their purpose already clearly defined, and a hope that affiliation with the agency will help
them to fulfill that purpose. But many groups in social
agencies are formed from small nuclei of individuals of
like age or interests. In such cases, as a collection of individuals begins through shared experience to develop
some feeling as a group unit, a common purpose emerges.
There can be no actual group purpose until the members
of a group have had enough experience together that some
collective sense of goal can develop.

A distinction is made between the total of individual
purposes of those persons who comprise the group and
the common group purpose. People join groups with
widely varied hopes, some of which may be fulfilled in the
actual group experience. As the individual becomes part
of the group, he may have to yield some of his original,
personal purpose to the emerging group purpose; or he
finds that his sense of purpose in belonging to a group
contributes to the fusion of his separate aims into a collective aim, and that his purpose is so closely identified with
what the group accepts as common, that both are strength-
ened. Group purpose, therefore, is more than the sum of
the purposes of its members, as the group is indeed more
than its members added together to make a whole. For
the members are in interacting relation to each other, and
thus their collective purpose is the result of the interchange in which every person may have a part in its definition and modification. Consensus is not essential and perhaps not even desirable, since differences are valued.[26]

But there must be a degree of acceptance of a common goal if the group is to move forward.

Both expressed and unexpressed purposes are the group worker's concern. The stated purposes may be in general terms, such as: "to have fun," "to improve our neighborhood"; or they may be quite specific and limited, as: "to have a team," "to raise money for the Day Camp," "to have parties with boys." As one seventeen-year-old boy expressed it: "We used to be just a basketball team and never did anything else, and that's why we were together. Lately we've been branching out and inviting other groups, just girls, down to our place and having parties, etc.—kind of going in for the social stuff." This kind of informal statement of group purpose is very familiar to workers, formulated by one member, speaking either for himself or for the group.

One eighty-year-old man's poignant expression of individual purpose for being a club member carried the feeling shared by all of his fellow members. He wrote for the club newspaper: "I look forward to each Tuesday when I can visit our 'Old Cronies Club.' It is like a holiday for me; it is something to look forward to and not just another day. I come to our club for entertainment and to meet old cronies like myself—old and dear friends." In more collective terms, members of a boys' "street-corner" club in a settlement neighborhood have been heard by their worker to say: "We want the club to be a square bunch of guys that will be welcomed no matter where we go." And in more preventive terms: "We don't want to get a 'rep' for being wise guys." From such statements by the members, the worker forms his idea of the group's deeper purpose of seeking something new in responsible relationships to each other and society.

Occasionally, groups are formal enough in their procedures to have written statements of purpose. Club constitutions include statements of club purpose, which are written expressions of what the members believe their group to stand for. But when group members have not defined their collective purpose, or are not vocal about it, discussion initiated by the worker serves to clarify it both for the members and the worker. For while some group purposes are freely expressed, others, often more fundamental, are unacknowledged by words, and the worker can only assume them from his knowledge of human needs. Need is not to be confused with purpose but, rather, as shaping and precipitating it. In the organization of one's self around a specific problem or interest, purpose to do something about it emerges, even though the problem is not fully acknowledged.

A distinction is sometimes made between group work and casework to the effect that the potential group member comes to the group work agency with little of the sense of personal problem or inadequacy that impels a client to seek the service of a casework agency. There may, indeed, be a great difference in the nature and urgency of the need, but the group work "client" must have some sense of need or he would not organize his will sufficiently to move out to an agency. Certainly the fundamental need of a person to be with other people of his own choosing, to be accepted by them and to find some degree of security with them, is operating and contributing to the individual's purpose in applying for membership in a group work agency.[27] He must be hoping for some fulfillment of his need to be relating to others who have some degree of likeness—some common bond—whether it be age, nationality, program interest, or ideas and attitudes. While this need may not be clearly expressed as the member comes to the agency, it is a universal need that the group worker may assume as real.

Group purposes, as defined and described above, must be taken into account by the worker. To disregard them is to shut off a rich source for the worker's understanding of membership. However, the worker's purpose, as he helps group members to use their group experience, is not identical with the group purpose. Indeed, the professional goal avowedly goes beyond the group members' goals for themselves and may, at points, be even contradictory to them. Although the group worker in leisure-time agencies deals with people who only in rare instances have come to the agency overtly seeking help or ask for it directly, he considers the purpose of his every contact with them to be to help them to use group experiences provided by the agency. Later discussion will reveal that the worker does not force his "help," but engages the person to be helped in a process which has strong elements of the group member's own choosing. While the worker's specific goals for his work with groups and their individual members must be kept constantly fluid, shifting in the context of the process with the groups, still a well-defined, constant direction, given him by identification with professional and agency goals, must lie clearly before the worker.

Professional goals may well encompass the group's goals, and the difference between them may lie only in the interpretation of the goal and the method by which it can be approached. Thus, the group work professional purpose is more comprehensive than the group purpose, for the aim of *helping* is fundamental to it. Professional purpose, with which the worker must be identified as he encompasses the more specific agency and group goals, implies, then, a method as well as a goal. Skill in using the method can be developed only as the worker focuses consistently on the purpose for which it is being used.

Conscious group work skill, like purpose, has gone through an evolutionary development, and we will turn next to an examination of its growth, followed by identification of some of the values that underlie it.

CHAPTER NOTES

1. The term "social group work" came into general use in the thirties. While the term is now almost universally used by practitioners and educators, it has not been adopted by some who prefer the term "informal group education." "Social group work" will be used exclusively throughout this writing to indicate a method of working with groups, and the term "group workers" to describe, somewhat anachronistically, those persons whose efforts have been directed to working with leisure-time groups, at whatever historical period.

2. The Young Men's Christian Association of this country was organized in Boston in 1851.

   The first Young Men's Hebrew Association was established in Baltimore in 1854, although similar organizations under different names antedate it by four years, the first of which was the Young Men's Literary Association of Philadelphia.

The Young Women's Christian Association appeared in Boston in 1866, following eight years of experimentation with associations under various titles.

The Neighborhood Guild (now called University Settlement), organized in 1886 in New York City, was the first social settlement to be established in this country.

3. Evidences of the connection between social work and settlement work are to be found in histories of the settlement movement; autobiographies and biographies of the settlement pioneers, e.g., Jane Addams, Lillian Wald, Graham Taylor; papers in the proceedings of the Conference of Charities and Corrections (later the National Conference of Social Work), from 1894 to the present time.

4. F. G. Peabody, "Social Settlements," *Conference of Charities and Corrections,* XXIV, 1897, p. 330.

5. *Ibid.*

6. Robert A. Woods and Albert J. Kennedy, *The Settlement Horizon* (New York: Russell Sage Foundation, 1922), p. 28.

7. Gertrude Wilson and Gladys Ryland, *Social Group Work Practice* (Boston: Houghton Mifflin, 1949) comment on the slow development of social agencies. "They [the pioneer leaders] focused their attention upon the service to be given and not upon the establishment of agencies . . .," p. 12.

8. Jane Addams, "Social Settlements," *Conference of Charities and Corrections,* XXIV, 1897, p. 389.

9. John McDowell and participants in the Cleveland Settlement Study, "Foreword and Statement of Purposes and Functions of Settlements in Cleveland," 1946.

10. For example, the garment workers were first organized into trade unions through the encouragement of the Hull House workers in the early nineties.

11. Vida D. Scudder, "Settlement Past and Future," Denison House College Settlement Report, 1900.

12. John Lovejoy Elliott, "After Twenty Years in the Tenement Houses of New York." Address given in New York City before the Society of Ethical Culture, April 11, 1915.

13. Harriet Vittum, "Politics from the Social Point of View," *Proceedings of the National Conference of Social Work,* LI, 1924, pp. 422–428.

14. Francis Bosworth, "Settlements and Neighborhood Centers," *Social Work Year Book* (New York: American Association of Social Workers, XII, 1954), pp. 471–472.

UNIVERSITY *of* PENNSYLVANIA
SCHOOL OF SOCIAL WORK
2410 PINE STREET, PHILADELPHIA, PA. 19103

Date

From

To

15. Johan Grolle, Symposium on "Settlement Goals for the Next Third of a Century" (New York: National Federation of Settlements, 1926), p. 29.
16. Much later, during the depression of the 1930's, settlements were able to provide extensive and effective opportunities for experience with cultural arts through the assignment to them of leaders through the Works Progress Administration of the Federal government.
17. Robert A. Woods, "The Settlement's Foothold of Opportunity," a communication sent to the First International Conference of Settlements at London, July, 1922; published in Robert A. Woods, *The Neighborhood in Nation-building* (Boston: Houghton Mifflin, 1923), p. 310.
18. Grace L. Coyle, in "Changing Perspectives in the Development of Group Work," *The Jewish Center,* September, 1942, discusses the relation of group work to progressive education and psychoanalysis.
19. Helen Hart, "The Changing Function of the Settlement under Changing Conditions," *Proceedings of the National Conference of Social Work,* LVIII (Chicago: University of Chicago Press, 1931), pp. 291–292.
20. Julia C. Lathrop, "Hull House as a Sociological Laboratory," *National Conference of Charities and Corrections,* XXI, 1894, p. 315.
21. Wilber I. Newstetter, "What Is Social Group Work?" *Proceedings of the National Conference of Social Work,* LXII, 1935, p. 291.
22. Grace L. Coyle, "Social Group Work," *Social Work Year Book,* IV, 1937, p. 461.
23. Wilson and Ryland, *op. cit.,* p. 61.
24. The National Association for the Study of Group Work, organized in 1936, became the American Association of Group Workers in 1946 when it took on the characteristics of a professional association, with membership requirements related to professional training and experience. In 1955, the American Association of Group Workers merged with five other professional associations to form a single body—the National Association of Social Workers. A group work section is provided for the pursuance of the distinct activities and interests of group workers.
25. American Association of Group Workers Committee Report, "Definition of the Function of the Group Worker," *The Group,* XI, May, 1949, p. 11.

26. Nathaniel Cantor, in "Focus and Function in Group Discussion," *Teachers College Record*, LIII, April, 1952, pp. 375–382, emphasizes this point.

27. Grace L. Coyle, in "The Contribution of Group Experience to the Development of Older Children," *Proceedings of the National Conference of Social Work*, LXVIII, 1941, p. 68, discusses illuminatingly the needs of adolescents that can be met by social group work.

CHAPTER II

The Development and Nature of Social
Group Work Skill: Its Philosophic Base

FROM OUR CONSIDERATION of the development of professional purpose it is apparent that, through several generations, those people who chose to devote their lives to
the leadership of leisure-time and informal educational
groups were motivated by a desire to help the members
of those groups to find richer lives for themselves. By implication, one could judge that the methods and skill for
achieving such a goal developed from the beginnings
made by people who wanted to help. As social situations
changed, as psychological and sociological insights increased, methods for helping people use their group experiences were slowly transformed from the trial-and-
error approach of intelligent and socially minded group
leaders, building soundly on their past experience, to the
conscious and disciplined approach of the skilled group
worker of the present day.

GROWTH OF INTEREST IN SKILL

An index to the growth of interest in group work methodology is to be found in the data concerning the establishment, in schools of social work, of training programs for social group work in which skill in using the group work method could be acquired. Several valuable precursors to these programs were operating in the twenties. Notable among them were the Recreation Training School, directed by Neva Boyd, located first in the School of Civics and Philanthropy of Chicago and later in Northwestern University; a specialization in Group and Community Leadership at Teachers College of Columbia University; George Williams and Springfield Colleges, established by the National Young Men's Christian Association as training schools for workers for their Association; [1] and the National Recreation Training School, conducted by the National Recreation Association. The first Masters' degrees to be granted by a university to group work students in a school of social work were given to graduates of what was called the "Group Service" curriculum at the School of Applied Social Sciences at Western Reserve University in 1926. By 1943, fifteen schools of social work were known by the American Association of Schools of Social Work to be offering preparation for social group work and, in 1950, twenty-one group work specializations had been approved by the accreditation commission of that organization. This number increased to twenty-five in 1954, dropped to twenty-three in 1955, and stands at twenty-four in 1956.[2] The contribution of group work agency executives and practitioners to the development of group work education has been active and constant since its inception.[3]

The body of knowledge taught in the earlier group work courses was borrowed widely from other disciplines and fields while this specialization of the social work profession was in the process of discovering its own identity. Reading lists for group work courses were heavily weighted with the writings of Dewey, Kilpatrick, Watson, MacIver, Thrasher, and Eubank—educators, social psychologists, and sociologists. Indeed, for several years both the methods and principles of progressive education were drawn on and consciously applied to work with leisure-time groups as the direction for group work practice.

From the field of recreation, group workers absorbed many skills related to the area of program activities and the development of community-wide recreational programs. Due to the earnest efforts of some of the leaders in both group work and recreation, an early competition between the two has been practically eliminated, with the general agreement that recreation be considered as a field of activity, and group work as a method which may be used in many settings, including the field of recreation.[4]

In the early stages of the group workers' acknowledgment that their practice was part of the larger profession of social work, there was a tendency to absorb everything possible of insight from social casework. This was during the period when caseworkers were intensely interested in psychiatry, eventuating in a struggle to define their method of helping as distinct from psychotherapy. This struggle influenced the group workers' search for the separate identity of their method. The slowness with which group workers found and claimed the uniqueness of their method is partially accounted for by the fact that, without exception, professional training for social group work was introduced into schools of social work with well-established curricula in social casework. Thus, for many years, most schools of social work required the group work students to carry courses in social casework method, often accompanied by field work, with the implication that only so could they understand the dynamics of human behavior or acquire professional social work skill. It must be admitted that group workers, always in the minority in social work faculties as well as in the social work community, tended to be somewhat defensive about their specialization, attempting to prove the professional quality of it by seeking for its likenesses to casework. Due to the long-continuing efforts of both educators and practitioners, often centered in committees of the American Association of Schools of Social Work and of the American Association of Group Workers, a generic base for social work practice and education for it has been articulated with clear-cut definition of specializations, of which social group work is a distinct entity.

The uniqueness of social group work stems from the purpose of this segment of the social work profession—to help people use group experiences for their self-growth toward social ends. The distinguishing characteristic of the group work method, therefore, lies in its emphasis on group relations—its inevitable identification with the interacting process between group members, consciously stimulated and directed by a worker.[5] Thus, in 1949, two group work educators wrote: "We therefore see social group work as a process and a method through which group life is affected by a worker who consciously directs the interacting process toward the accomplishment of goals which in our country are conceived in a democratic frame of reference." [6] When, from the many contributing strands of knowledge from diverse disciplines and from the constant testing of concepts in practical experience, there emerged the discovery and definition of a unique group work method, the nature of the skill required to employ the method became increasingly apparent.

It would be both unfair and false to assume that group work skill originated with the introduction of training for social workers in schools of social work, for the idea of what constitutes skillful group work has developed steadily from the experience of several generations of workers. But the term "skill," in the discussion that follows, refers to a conscious, disciplined use of one's self and one's abilities which can be acquired reliably only through the disciplined experience of professional training for social group work, during which the potential group worker, as a student, not only takes help in his learning from teachers and supervisors, but carries responsibility in a group work agency simultaneous with his acquisition of group work theory as experienced in classes and field work.[7] At the end of his two years of professional training, the student is not expected to be truly skillful, but he is required to have gained what Dr. Wessel calls "a trustworthy degree

of sureness in the use of himself in relationships." For the
training, with its carefully defined focus and structures,
provides the student with an experience through which
he gradually acquires skill.

SOCIAL WORK VALUES

While purpose gives direction to skill, there are also fundamental values upon which the social group worker builds
his skill. The fundamental, unshakable value that under-
girds all of the helping professions is that every person in-
herently has the capacity to change, and that he himself
determines whether or in what way he will change in his
relationships to others. One of the clearest written statements to indicate the relation of this philosophic value to
social work practice is found in a paper of the late Kenneth L. M. Pray. Describing functional casework, he
wrote: ". . . the client, whatever his strengths and weak-
nesses, carries responsibility for his own life as a whole
and must continue to carry it. At least he has not asked us,
and we cannot consent, to take that responsibility from
him. He has asked us, rather, to help him to carry that
responsibility for helping him to overcome some obstacle
he has faced in carrying it, and in the very act of seeking
this help he has disclosed at least some elements of
strength for dealing with this responsibility. The worker's
task is to enable him to build on this latent strength, to
face whatever realities are decisive in determining his own
use of himself and of available resources in relation to the
problem he faces and upon which he wants to work. The
problem remains his own; the responsibility for dealing

with it remains with him. Furthermore, this approach
. . . also starts with the assumption—indeed, the profound
conviction—that the helping dynamic, the source of heal-
ing power, is also in the client himself as he reaches out
for help. It is not primarily in the worker." [8]

Such a professional credo recognizes the strength in people and the power of the human will to determine what
one will do in response to life's demands. But it also testi-
fies to the part that a professional helping person may have
in enabling one to discover and carry his responsible part
in relationships. This leads to a second major philosophic
base for social work, namely, that there are dynamic possibilities for growth in the process of interacting relationships. The process between members of a group and their
worker requires of the worker active engagement with
them as he carries his responsibility to help them use the
group experience for their social growth, both by enabling
them to develop the process of group relations and by
letting the outcome of the process be their own.

On the one hand are these philosophic values; on the
other are the professional purposes. These are the roots
of social group work skill. The capacity to translate values
into professional efforts that precipitate movement toward
the fulfillment of purpose constitutes social group work
skill. If the values of strength for self-determination and
growth through relationships are to be maintained in the
movement toward achieving purpose, the worker's efforts
will be concentrated on helping the members of his
groups to make responsible choices, to discover and claim

their responsibility for their attitudes and behavior in their relations to the group, the agency, and society.

To test the use of social group work skill for its effectiveness in achieving group work purpose, this one part of purpose—the development of responsible behavior—has been selected. What kind of skill is required of the worker if he is to help group members to increased accountability for their attitudes and actions? In what way does the use of social group work skill contribute to movement toward this purpose? These are the questions that will be considered in the following pages of Part Two, starting with exploration into the skill required to use the agency function.

CHAPTER NOTES

1. Both George Williams and Springfield Colleges are still in existence and have expanded their curricula to include a two-year graduate program in group work and community organization.
2. From material compiled by the Council on Social Work Education, formerly the American Association of Schools of Social Work, 1956.
3. The common concern of practitioners and educators for the content and quality of educational programs was channelized by the formation, in 1943, of an Advisory Committee to the Conference of Professional Schools of Recreation and Group Work. This committee, representing both professional schools and national agencies, has continued under various names and auspices until it is presently located in the Council on Social Work Education, as the Committee on Group Work.
4. In a paper given at the National Conference of Social Work at Buffalo in 1946, Grace Coyle said: "One of the confusions which has troubled those engaged in the field of recreation or informal education services is the relation between recreation and group work. It would seem that the clearest definition of that relation lies in the acceptance of recreation—or informal education—as functions to be performed or services to be rendered, and of group

work as one method of fulfilling these functions." *Proceedings of the National Conference of Social Work,* 1946; reprinted in *Group Experience and Democratic Values* (New York: Woman's Press, and Whiteside, 1947).

5. Chapter VI is devoted to an elaboration of this point.

6. Gertrude Wilson and Gladys Ryland, *Social Group Work Practice* (Boston: Houghton Mifflin, 1949), p. 61.

7. Dr. Wessel describes the relation of theory to practice in social work training as follows: "In the training experience in which I have been engaged as advisor and teacher [University of Pennsylvania School of Social Work] . . . the truly unique factor is the simultaneity of the development of skill in practice and the *experiencing* of the theory that underlies it. . . . It is this simultaneity that supplies the student with the core of what he must learn in practice—not an external content of techniques to be applied, but a knowing of himself in relationship, in a structured setting of time and place, as he takes help in his learning and as he gives it to his clients." "The Place of Practice in Education for Social Work," in the volume by Rosa Wessel and Goldie Basch Faith, *Professional Education Based in Practice* (Philadelphia: University of Pennsylvania School of Social Work, 1953), p. 64.

8. Kenneth L. M. Pray, "A Restatement of the Generic Principles of Social Casework," *Social Work in a Revolutionary Age* (Philadelphia: University of Pennsylvania Press, 1949), p. 249.

Part **TWO** | THE USE OF

SOCIAL GROUP

WORK SKILL

CHAPTER III

Skill in Using Agency Function

X **W**ITH CONSIDERATION for the professional purpose and basic values of social work, group work agencies have defined the scope of their activities and services—the specific agency function. Social agency function is the service developed and offered to the community as a means of carrying out the agency's purpose.

THE GROUP WORK AGENCY FUNCTION

The function of the group work agency is to provide group experiences—the kind of group experience that, through

Wherever the term "agency function" appears in the pages that follow, reference is made both to agencies whose sole service is group work and to the group services or group work departments which may be only part of an agency's total service. In the latter category are multifunctional agencies, such as settlements and neighborhood houses, and host agencies (e.g., hospitals, clinics, residential treatment centers), in which group work services may be located. To avoid awkwardness of expression and to emphasize the importance of agency-based service, "agency function," without qualifying words, will be used throughout this chapter.

appropriate structures and enabling leadership, will contribute to the fulfillment of the agency's purposes of ef-
fecting the social growth of the groups' participants and
the development of group units in the direction of social
usefulness. The constant demand on the worker as he
helps the members to develop both themselves as individuals and their groups is that he focus his attention on
the group relations which the agency provides by its very
function. The group unit is the primary working base for
the worker's contribution to the fulfillment of agency purpose.

To use the reality of the agency function helpfully for
group members requires understanding of the relation of
the part to the whole—of the possibilities for personal
growth in one's relation to the group of which he is part—
with the conviction, already presented as a philosophic
base of group work,[1] that one can move toward a wholeness in himself through relationships with others. Personal movement toward wholeness may, indeed, obtain
in a group that meets without the presence of a group
worker. But a worker, using himself consciously to effect change in the group relationships and representing an
agency whose function he carries, both accelerates and
gives direction to the process of group relationships. Part
of his direction stems from his understanding and acceptance of the agency's function.

Trecker emphasizes this point in his discussion of
agency function, which, he says, "should be regarded as a
positive tool which the worker can use with his groups.
. . . Groups must be helped to see, understand, and accept

both the opportunities and the limits implied in the agency purpose and setting. As a representative of the agency, the group worker is constantly called upon to interpret and reinterpret agency function, and his own job in relation to it. Without the understanding which emerges from such a process, it is doubtful whether or not groups can relate satisfactorily to the agency for a very long time." [2]

The skillful worker carries the function in himself, not needing to protest it by words, but directing all of his efforts consistently toward what the agency is in the community to do, and contributing to the doing of it. To find and take direction from the agency function is at once both supporting and liberating to the worker, giving him, as it does, a foundation and clear focus for his work.

In actual practice at present, not all professional group workers subscribe to the limited group-centered focus herein described. More inclusive efforts at helping are practiced, seemingly in the belief that a wide variety of individualized services can be anticipated to help agency members use their group experiences more fully, and that therefore they fall within the function of the group work agency. This question will be considered in some detail later in this chapter. Suffice it to say here that the group worker's problem of finding a balance between group and individual contacts is a persistent one. It is the writer's opinion that this problem can be met comfortably only as the worker keeps his focus on the primary group-centered function of his agency.

Since we are claiming that consciously using the agency

function is essential to social group work skill, we will focus, in this chapter, on the way in which the worker can use the agency function as a starting point for the development of an unfolding process between the group and himself that moves toward fulfillment of group work purpose. We will consider the nature of the beginning and continuing process through which the members comprehend and relate to the agency function; the elements of choice in the process that further in the members the quality of social responsibility.

THE INTAKE PROCESS

For most group members, the initial point of the process of becoming related to a leisure-time agency comes at the time when the person appears at the doors of the agency to signify his interest in "joining" a club, or team, or class, or troop. In some agencies, the response to such requests consists of little more than letting the inquirer sign up for activities he would like to take part in. But in an increasing number of agencies, a well-defined intake process has grown out of careful deliberation and experimentation, with awareness of the significance of the initial contact, or of the renewed approach at the beginning of a program year, to the quality of the ongoing relationship to the agency.

The inner motivations of potential members as they seek admission to an agency are varied. The applicant may come in with some of his friends who have told him of the agency or who, like him, are curious about what may be there for them. If he is a child, he may have been

urged by his parents to join the agency, or it may have
been a caseworker who has suggested this step to him. For
some there is the interest of being with familiar friends;
for others, the opportunity to establish new friendships.
For all, whatever the particular motivation, there is the
intent of finding something for one's self, whether or not
it is clearly defined and expressed.

The worker who meets the applicant, while carrying
out the agency's procedures for intake, will discuss with
him what he particularly wants from the agency as well
as what is available there for him to consider—both the
privileges and responsibilities of agency membership. Obviously, this calls for something more than a knowledge of
the agency's program schedule and membership fees; it
requires a clear idea of what the agency is there to do.
This knowledge can be conveyed to the applicant in a
number of ways. For example, as he says that he wants to
join a group or a number of groups, he finds that there
are many groups served in this agency, that he can choose
a limited number for his own participation, but that the
agency is there for *groups,* not exclusively for the one or
two to which he will belong. This possibility becomes
clear as the worker and member work together on the
concrete fact of the days of the week and hours of the day
that the agency is available to him.

That the agency serves people in groups, rather than
primarily by individual counseling, can be clear at the
outset if the discussion is kept focused on the activities
and groups that are possible for the applicant. If the
agency is sought initially for help with some expressed

problem of personal relationships, the worker will share whatever information he possesses regarding the appropriate agencies in the community whose function is to work with people who have the problem indicated, thereby implying what the group work agency does or does not do.[3]

Whatever the specific content of the intake interview, the worker will need to be sensitive to the possible mixed feelings of purposefulness and apprehension in the applicants before him, knowing that part of his own purpose in the interview is to meet their feeling as he helps them to define more clearly what they are seeking from the agency and to choose the part of the agency's service that they can use.

If an applicant is not familiar with the agency and its members, he has mustered a good deal of strength to approach its doors, and he is indicating that he is ready, at least to some degree, to risk himself in new relationships, or he would not have come. In a very real sense, the member, as he takes this first step of joining the agency, commits himself to some kind of engagement with others—not irretrievably so, for it is inevitable that the choice to use the agency's services will have to be made again and again—but he has expressed his interest in being part of the agency and its groups, and has taken an initial step toward using the services of the agency.

From the application interview will result, for the applicant, a beginning sense of the way the agency gives its service. He finds that his interests and needs are taken into account and responded to; that he is helped to choose if he wants the agency service, and to select the part of it that he wants, within the limitations of the agency structures; that there are certain agency expectations of its membership, such as meeting with a worker whom the agency provides. Most important of all the aspects of the intake process is the feeling tone established, not always conveyed by words, that gives the applicant an experience in what the agency is like; for at the point of intake, the worker is the agency for the applicant. The process of relationship between member and agency begins here with the intake worker, although it may well be continued with another worker. And from the nature of the intake interview, the potential member can gain the sense that here is a service where he will be engaged in a process with an agency worker as well as with other group members. The worker can help an applicant acquire a beginning comprehension of the agency only if he possesses in himself a clear sense of its function.

Connecting the Group with the Agency

The content for this process of exploring and testing what the agency is like is apt to be some specific agency requirement or policy that, in a realistic way, affects the members' choice as to whether they will use the agency. The following account of the first meeting of a teen-age boys' club with a student worker, new to the club and the agency, presents us with a situation to be examined for the elements of choice and testing in an initial meeting. The group is composed of fourteen boys of the ages of fifteen to seventeen—a neighborhood friendship club with one year's affiliation with a large Center in an urban community which includes several ethnic groups. Due to staff interest and experimentation over a period of several years, the agency has developed clearly defined policies and structures governing membership practices. Among these practices is an agency ruling that requires members to register with the agency and to pay at least part of the agency membership fee before attending a meeting.

A few days before the meeting here recorded, the director of the agency's Youth Division had interviewed the boys as a group when they came into the agency together to find out if they could have their club at the Center a second season. The Division head made it quite clear to the boys that the agency would welcome them as part of it again, but that there were certain things expected of agency members. He referred to their previous year's experience at the Center, their failure to pay the requested membership fee and their generally destructive behavior. Because of this conduct, the staff had agreed that they might have a probationary period of six weeks this fall. During this time the boys would have to consider whether they wanted enough to be part of the agency to meet the requirements that were made of all agency members. The first step would be for them to make at least partial payment of their membership dues before they could hold their first meeting of the season, which they were requesting for the following week. Before the boys left the building they were introduced to the young man who would be their worker for the current program year, and together they set the date for the meeting. Now they gather for their first meeting on the appointed evening.

The group was due in the agency at 8:30 and I had barely returned to my office after a fruitless look for them in the lobby when one of the boys, Ed, burst into the office and asked me if I was going to meet with them. I said that I was, and started to walk down to the lobby with him. I was about to ask him if he had received permission to come upstairs, when the receptionist appeared and told Ed to go back to the lobby, helping him along with a little push. Ed started to flare up, and I took him gently by the arm and reminded him that he was really in the wrong and should not have run by the receptionist, even though I appreciated his eagerness to get the meeting started. He relaxed and we proceeded to the lobby.

The group, apparently fluctuating between lobby and street, gathered around me and said "hello." I sat down in a lobby chair and said I was glad to see everyone as eager for the first meeting as I myself was. The boys then physically indicated their willingness to start by moving toward the stairs. I just sat and smiled and they moved back. I told them I would like to check their membership cards before we went any further. This resulted in their playfully showing me all kinds of cards—driver's licenses, student organization cards from school, etc. After some questioning, it appeared that only one of the boys, Art, had gone through the registration procedure and paid his fee. I shook my head sadly, and said I was really sorry that we couldn't start meeting this week, but we would have to wait until registration and fee payment were taken care of. This was met with anguished cries, and Sam shyly asked me to "be a good guy" and take them upstairs anyway. We both laughed at this and I deliberately acted as if he were simply joking.

They went on to demand a hearing before Mr. K., the supervisor, on this subject. I said that Mr. K. was not in the building, but that since I was new in the agency, I would check up on the rule with another staff member to make sure I had the correct information. I asked them to wait while I went upstairs. The Division head agreed with me that since the boys had been informed of the deadline for making payments, they should not come into the building for a meeting tonight, but he suggested that I meet with them briefly on the street outside the building to try to set up a program with them for the following week.

When I returned to the lobby, I found that the boys had already retreated to the street. Art met me questioningly, and I said the decision stood as before. I joined the boys out in front and told them there was no change in the rule. Sam directed the group's attention across the street, where Ed was engaged in conversation with an older boy. Sam said, "If he bothers Ed, let's jump him." I turned to Sam and asked if it wouldn't be fairer to Ed to keep an eye on him so as to help him stay out of trouble. The older boy went on his way, Ed returned to the group, and Sam let my comment go without reply.

I took up my post against a parked car and tried to get some kind of discussion going. The boys milled around aimlessly and noisily without stopping or settling their attention on me or any other object. One of the boys expressed an obscene and hostile remark against the Division head. I told him he could take up his feelings about Mr. O. with Mr. O. if he wished, but that I couldn't accept this kind of talk as accomplishing anything worth-while. He asked how we were to meet on the sidewalk when there were blizzards and rainstorms. I said that I, too, would rather be in a comfortable meeting-room, but the facilities of the agency required money to maintain and if they wanted to use these facilities, they would have to pay their fees as other members did.

I got Martin interested in telling me of the club's basketball team, and Art went into a lyrical description of the team's prowess and past triumphs. I brought out a schedule of the big All-City games for the year. . . .

This started the boys talking with the worker about what they might do together during the club season—travel to see games, arrange a schedule for their club team to play bastketball, invite girls to meetings and parties, and elect new officers at their next meeting. Although a few of the boys kept pushing to get to the poolroom, most of them started to get interested in program ideas.

After the worker had written down the names of both present and absent members—

Martin and Art volunteered that they would all definitely pay up their dues by next week so that they could start in. I told them I looked forward to having a meeting next week. Martin said "Good-by" in a fairly friendly manner and I went back into the agency while they went on to the poolroom, or so I gathered was their intent.

This is a group which deliberately chose to come back to the agency for a second program year; at least they had moved as far as to come around to the building. But they still had reservations, for at this meeting they had not yet committed themselves to a clear enough choice to be part of the agency to motivate them to meet the first agency requirements which they well knew, both from their previous experience and the group intake interview. Here was a new worker who, perhaps, would not firmly be the agency, who might be willing to ignore the agency requirements and help them organize a basketball team on their terms. At least it was worth trying, and these boys used their first meeting with him to test his relation to the agency and to discover his expectation of their relation to it. What they met was someone who seemed warmly interested in them but who held them to choose whether they wanted enough to become part of the agency to meet the initial requirements. He responded with warmth to their testing out of him and the agency, at the same time that he made it clear to them that there were certain agency limits that he hoped they could meet.

The worker may have had some question about the agency requirement, but if he did, he kept his integrity even though disagreeing with the policy, for he did not disassociate himself from the agency. A disciplined worker faced with the dilemma of disagreeing with a policy to which he must hold a group seeks for the value in the policy and questions it responsibly through appropriate channels as he keeps his identification with the agency and its policies.

In this instance the worker's firmness was not presented in a demanding way that would have antagonized the boys. There must have been something in his manner that conveyed his concern for them as well as the objective evi-

dence of it, given them by his willingness to meet on the
street with them, his suggestions of ideas for program, and
by his rational explanation of the agency rule they were
resisting. Possibly he attempted to be too factual and rea-
sonable, and he might have been more helpful to them at
this point if he had recognized more openly their resistance to paying the agency fees. His clarity about what responsibility both the agency and he expected them to
assume, however, gave them something practical and concrete on which to base a decision about agency membership for themselves. He left the decision up to them, and
at the end of their few minutes together they moved tentatively toward the agency, allowing their spokesmen to de-
clare their intention to pay up their dues before another
week had passed.

The worker made a slight start in conveying to the boys
his expectation that something could change in their attitudes that would lead to more responsible behavior. Instead of encouraging a fight, could they keep one of their
members from engaging in one? If they felt hostile toward
another staff member, could they take it directly to him
instead of complaining irresponsibly about him to others?

Part of the growing skill of this student-worker lay in
his feeling of connection with the agency and his effort to
face the club members with a specific aspect of the agency
structure—payment of fees—and to engage them in a process of choice regarding that structure, which would be a
responsible step toward using the agency service.

Factually, the boys heard a little of the financial obliga-
tion of members, and that the agency was there to serve

many groups, all of whom are expected to assume similar obligations. But, more importantly, from this experience with their new worker they must have gained a sense that at this agency they could expect to have a worker who is a definite part of the agency, who is concerned enough about them as persons to question their attitudes and hold them to responsible behavior, who will help them to develop a program of activities to their liking and who, enabling them to make their own choices, expects them, in their group life in the agency, to take a responsible part which he will help them achieve.

Although the boys seemed close to making the choice of moving into the agency at the end of their first meeting, it is inevitable that they will continually, throughout the year, be faced with choices regarding their relation to the agency, with the expectation that they will take progressively responsible steps toward fuller use of the agency.

We have been considering the beginning of the process between group members and their worker. As experience together continues through regularly scheduled meetings into the sustaining phase of the process, frequent opportunities and demands occur for the worker to put into words the purpose of the agency, and to interpret something of the way it operates as it affects the group's interests.

When a group is under the auspices of an agency but meets outside the agency building, it is especially important that the worker use every available opportunity to relate the group to the agency of which it is a physically remote part.[4] Since there is no visible reminder of the affiliation, other than the worker provided by the agency, the worker must feel his own firm connection with the agency, and be alert to every occasion in which he may interpret to the group the function of the agency that is making his leadership services available to it. The very first contact with an out-of-building group, as well as with a building-centered group, sets the direction for the kind of use of the agency that the group members can achieve. Group workers have discovered the dynamic possibilities of using rather than hiding their agency affiliation. To present one's self as "just someone interested in boys" is likely to become an immediate target for suspicion, or to establish a casual, personal kind of relationship from which it is difficult to move, depriving the group of the richness of experience that can result from identifying with the larger whole of an agency, with its definition and scope that provide realities for the development of self and social responsibility.

The brief excerpt from a worker's record, presented below, describes part of a meeting of a settlement house staff-member with a group of teen-age boys who meet away from the agency building. It is included here for the worker's explicit interpretation of the function of the agency. The worker had first met the boys when he stopped at the steps of a corner-store where they were playing cards, introducing himself as a worker from the local settlement house. After some preliminaries regarding the kinds of activities they liked, he talked with them about the possibilities of meeting regularly with him once a week, if a meeting-place could be arranged. In the next two contacts with the worker, the boys decided they would like to establish themselves as a club with a leader and a regular meeting-place. Later, the worker, through a careful process of interpretation of the settlement's purpose and function to the priest of a local Roman Catholic church, obtained the use of one of the rooms of the parish house, in which the boys then met regularly. Their meetings consisted of developing club structures, planning and executing parties with girls, taking well-planned trips, and discussing their problems of dating and their attitudes toward their own race and others. Now, after three months of club experience, they were invited to attend a movie at the settlement house with other teen-age groups affiliated there.

. . . Luke asked if it wasn't next week that they were to go to the Neighborhood House. This precipitated a discussion of the movie and the House. Hank wondered about going down there since it was a pretty tough place. My question of his worry brought out their feeling that the Neighborhood House was the hangout for the Porter's Alley gang. I wondered if it was as bad as all that, but Milt said, "That Gooseman is bad enough!" There was a thorough discussion of Gooseman, leader of the gang, and the reputation of the Neighborhood House. I told them that all kinds of people came to the House, but when they came there they respected the House and there were no gang fights and nobody violated the fact that the House belonged to everybody in the neighborhood.

I took the chance to tell them what a settlement house is, that it is financed by the Community Chest, which is everybody's money, and so everybody has the right to use it. And I hoped they could see how they were using the House themselves through my leadership of their club and their occasional use of the facilities and equipment of the House. There seemed to be a growing understanding of this, and they finally began to ridicule the tough reputation of "Gooseman" and his gang, and said they certainly would be there on Tuesday. . . .

One might grant that the worker's statement that everyone was welcome in the agency because of the Community Chest support was somewhat misleading, as though there were no agency policies governing eligibility for membership. But the essential welcoming quality of the agency, coupled with its expectation that the members, too, would accept other groups they found there, was conveyed to these boys who had a question and problem that was real to them. Could the worker assure them that there would be no gang fights, or that, if confronted by a "tough" gang, they would be protected? That, the worker could not do—not in the terms that they might have wished; but he could and did assure them of the agency's expectation that there would be no gang fights, and that the groups that come there "respect the House."

It was an opportunity to let these particular boys, relatively new to the agency, know what was expected of them, as well as to feel the kind of support available to them. The boys seem to have begun to comprehend that the agency was in their neighborhood for many kinds of groups, and that it offered its services with the expectation that the groups who used them would respond to the agency philosophy of respecting the rights of others, gaining something for themselves in the process. The worker

was relating the group more firmly to the agency by helping them to understand what the agency stands for and
what kind of responsible behavior was expected of them
as well as of other groups.

SERVING THE INDIVIDUAL
THROUGH THE GROUP WORK PROCESS

The group work agency function of serving individuals
through groups demands that the worker direct his attention to every member's use of the group experience. Additional contacts with individual members between group
meetings are often desirable and necessary, but the common, shared group experience must be the focus of the
worker's help. Since the function of the agency includes
helping group units to develop in socially useful ways, as
well as helping individuals, the worker's attention must
simultaneously be on the development of the group as a
whole, and on each individual's use of the group.[5] Only
the conviction that these two movements are reciprocal
makes this duality possible for the worker.

Competence and self-responsibility accrue to a group
member who feels he contributes to the group something
valued by the other members. Conversely, as one seeks for
the value in a fellow member and learns to accept what he
brings to the group, even if it is different from the usual
pattern of participating members, there is gain for the
self, especially as this experience is shared by his colleagues.

The worker, concentrating on the development of the
group as the function of his agency requires him to do,
helps every member to find his part in the group as the

group develops through relationships. The practice recorded below describes a worker's efforts to help a need-
ful adolescent boy within the process of the meetings of
the group as he simultaneously helps the group as a
whole.

The club is a friendship group of Negro boys, sixteen
and seventeen years old, who for a number of years have
been meeting together in an interracial settlement house.
Carl, who figures prominently in the excerpted records
presented here, is mentally slower than the other boys,
and the only one of them who has attended one of the
city's special schools for mentally retarded children. In
the previous year Carl's participation in meetings was
limited to silly and irrelevant remarks, which other members either laughed at or criticized, depending on the
seriousness of the discussion. His part in club projects was
characterized by lack of co-operation and responsibility,
except when the boys forced him into the position of a
scapegoat. However, at the beginning of a new club season Carl is looking for acceptance from the others in a
different way.

At the first club meeting in the fall, the boys decided
to elect a new president and after discussing what they
wanted of a president, they began to consider candidates.

. . . Carl, who had been waving his hand around for some
time, was called on by Caleb, last year's president, who was
chairing the meeting. He stood up and talked at length in
a rambling way, saying that he had never had a job with
the club except washing dishes at camp; therefore, he
thought he ought to be president. There was a lot of laugh-

ter from the group and Carl laughed with them, but I felt
that there was real feeling behind what Carl said, and that
the laughter hurt. I said nothing at this point, not wanting
to influence the elections unduly.

Caleb asked for nominations, and Sonny nominated
Dougie, whom John seconded. Duffy laughingly nominated
Carl—"because he is my good friend and we work together."
After a lot of kidding, Joe seconded the nomination. They
decided to vote by a show of hands. Carl and Dougie were
asked to leave the room. Carl flashed a small razor at the
group as he went out, and laughed. When Caleb took a poll
of each one, the vote was three to one, favoring Dougie,
before coming to John. John said that since it didn't make
any difference in the outcome, he would vote for Carl. They
called Carl in first, and he said he knew something was
wrong. Caleb told him the outcome and all of the boys
were quite explicit in telling him that it had been a very
close vote. . . .

Later when Dougie, the newly elected president, asked
for nominations for the vice-president, John suggested Carl,
amid much less laughter than before. There were several
remarks supporting this suggestion. At the call for a vote,
all hands were raised in favor of Carl. Carl responded by
saying that it didn't mean anything to be vice-president because Dougie would always be there anyway, and he left
the meeting ten minutes later. . . .

From this account of part of a meeting, it appears that
the worker was not vocally active in the discussion regarding the election, but he was using himself consciously.
He deliberately refrained from speaking while nominees
were being considered, knowing that it was acceptance

from the boys, rather than from him, that Carl really wanted and needed, and that he could not protect him from the hurt of losing the election. The boys, perhaps guilty for their previous ridicule of their fellow member, showed considerable sensitivity to him in their announcement of the outcome of the vote and in their genuine willingness to make him vice-president, thus showing some concern for his feelings and evidence of beginning responsibility to a member whom they did not value highly. Here, the worker might well have helped Carl by recognizing his disappointment and anger over the loss of the presidency, but he wisely refrained from trying to build up the job of vice-president to Carl, who knew that this second position was not coveted by the club members.

The process of working with members continues in successive weekly meetings, and at the next meeting of this group there was opportunity for the worker to help this troubled boy find a more responsible and valued place in his club. The worker records:

> . . . A discussion about boxing followed. The boys know much more about this sport than I do, and knowing Carl's interest and ability in boxing, I encouraged him to take an active part. He seemed to take a great deal of satisfaction from his part in the conversation. The climax came for him when Norman, who is undergoing special training and is reputedly the best boxer in the club, said: "When it comes to boxing, Carl sure knows a lot!"

Here, the worker, aware of Carl's special needs, helped him talk about something in which he felt adequate, and

since it was a subject that was important to the whole
club, he was meeting simultaneously both Carl's need for
acceptance and the group's interest. A week later came
Carl's chance to chair the meeting in his office of vice-
president, and the worker's chance to help him take on
his new and threatening responsibilities:

I had a short talk with John before anyone else had arrived. One of the things he told me was that Dougie would
not be present today and that Carl would be taking charge.
When the rest of the fellows came in, it was evident that
Carl was all set to chair the meeting. He said something
about the meeting getting started and Duffy kidded him
about not knowing how to start it. I suggested quietly to
him: "Just say that the meeting is called to order." He did
this, and added: "Hats off!" Three or four who had not
taken off their hats did so and only Caleb kept his on.

In response to Carl's request for business, several responded with points of interest at the same time. Carl
called out that he would start around the table and call on
each member in turn. He called on Duffy first, who asked
me about a trip to camp. . . . In the midst of a lively discussion of camp I realized that Carl, with great concern,
was asking John to get charge of the meeting again. John
shook his head. I called a halt to the discussion and said
that Carl wished to speak. Carl said everyone was talking
without his calling on them. I said this was true and that I
had been at fault in this, too, but I thought we had all been
carried away by the thought of camp. Again Carl started
to call on people around the table. . . .

Later, when Caleb was called on, he said that Carl wasn't
doing any good and someone else should take his place. I

wondered why, and Caleb said that Carl was laughing too much. I said I thought the person in charge of a meeting couldn't be serious all of the time and could laugh like the other fellows. I continued that Carl was keeping good order and helping the meeting to move right along. Carl followed this by defending himself heatedly, and he and Caleb began to argue. Joe and John backed Carl vigorously. Duffy started to defend Caleb, suggesting they have another election. When I playfully asked what they thought about the national elections the next day, there was a wave of response. . . . (Discussion points that followed as Carl continued to call on the various members were: national elections, price controls, teen-age lounge, and basketball suits.)

Carl brought up the point that since they were a year older now, he thought they shouldn't swear about each other's families in meeting. There was some discussion but no real opposition. When Carl put his suggestion to a vote, it was passed, with only two dissenting votes. . . . After the meeting was over, I had a chance to see Carl and tell him I thought he had done a swell job of conducting the meeting.

Where was the worker's effort directed during this meeting? Obviously he was intent for the most part on helping the boy who felt uncertain of himself and his own place in the group to carry his particular responsibilities in a way that would be satisfying to him and acceptable to the other members. At one point he lost that focus, disregarding Carl during the discussion of camping, rather than helping him to take a chairman's part in a way that would not have interfered with the spontaneity of the other members. He quickly recovered, however, drawing the group's attention back to the vice-president whom they had elected, without rejecting them or their interest in camping. The function of his agency was to help individuals achieve an increasing sense of self-value and responsibility for their actions and thus to benefit from their group experience in the agency; his focus, therefore, was on the individual members and their needs as the process of the meeting developed. Carl himself had a great deal at stake in the meeting, the first one in which he was expected to preside at the meeting and to prove to his fellow members that he was capable even of being the president. He handled the meeting courageously in the only way he knew how to do it, by giving each member a turn to speak. The worker's support, verbalized at several spots, was helpful to him, and the growing acceptance of him by the other members made this support appropriate as it would not have been at the first meeting.

The situation of this meeting demanded that the worker help the member who seemed in the most need of help; but that help was rooted firmly in the group process, so that at no point was the relationship only between the worker and the boy. The worker could not support or accept Carl *for* the group; he could help the group to accept him in the actual experience together where relationships were being tested and developed. From this meeting all of the group members could gain the sense that they were with a worker and an agency that encouraged and helped each member to meet responsibilities given him by the club.

Every time a member is helped by the worker to come

to a decision with other members, to use a program activity with more satisfaction, to relate to others in a more responsible way—he is experiencing what the agency, through the worker, has to give him by way of service. The worker's active relation to the member is a significant part of the service but it is always subsidiary to the member's group relations; for the efforts of the worker whose focus is consonant with the agency's function are directed toward helping each member to benefit from the group relations and experience. Within the group setting the worker, sensitive to individual differences and needs, helps each member to use the group relations, the program of activities, and the relationship to himself, to find a new relation to his group and, hence, to living. He helps each member to use and, through experience with it, to comprehend the agency service or function.

WORKING WITH THE INDIVIDUAL
OUTSIDE THE GROUP MEETING

It has been stated in a number of ways in this chapter that part of the purpose of the group work agency is to help people to develop responsible relations in groups, and that its function is to offer group experiences under certain defined conditions. It follows that although the worker's help toward fulfilling the purpose is offered primarily within the group process, part of that help may be given through individual contacts with members, to the end that they may make better use of the group experience. The adjective used rather widely by group workers to describe these interviews as "marginal" indicates the close connection between the individual and group contact, placing the individual interview on the margin or the border of the group—not in isolation from it.

Perhaps the most controversial question in group work practice centers around the nature of the individual contact. What is the scope of the problems for which the group worker can offer and direct his help? What is the connection between the worker's help in an interview and the agency function? Pursuit of the second question may throw light on the first.

Individual interviews are initiated by either the worker or the group member. It is common group work practice for the worker to invite a club officer or committee member to talk with him about plans for the meetings or about how the member can carry out the responsibilities delegated to him by the group. Or, if a member is seen to have difficulty with program activity or his relationship with other group members, the worker often supplements what he does to help the member within the group setting by a private conversation with him about his group participation. These interviews are clearly related to the group experience, and therefore present no question as to whether or not they lie within the agency's function.

The combination of group and individual contact to help a member make better use of himself in his group participation is illustrated by the following partial recording of three consecutive meetings of a Junior boys' club and of a supplementary interview which the worker initiated.

. . . In the midst of working on their leather articles, Earl said to Ducky, "You better get off that table and get out of my face. Otherwise, I'm going to slug you one!" Ducky turned to him with, "You better not—I got friends." Earl said, "I'll take care of myself, no matter who I'm fighting." A real argument started and I interrupted by asking Earl if he was trying to get a reputation. (To these boys, a person has a "rep" when he is known never to back down on a fight and when he is famous for antisocial behavior.) Earl turned and said, "I don't care—I got one for busting windows in school, anyway." Cliff said, "You don't have one in this school, though," and Earl replied, "I don't care whether I do or I don't." I said I hoped he did care as I didn't think having a reputation was anything to brag about. Earl said, "That's all right. I just don't want anybody to think I'm going to back out." "You just watch yourself, Earl," Cliff, the president, said. "We're all in this same club—ain't nobody had anything against Earl but we just didn't see why he was trying to get a rep as that sure wouldn't help him any."

At the next week's meeting, Earl expressed hostility toward another one of the boys.

. . . While the dues were being collected, Henry said he was going to start making a leather wallet. Earl jumped on him and said, "You're always waiting until the last minute to do something. We'll be working on leather only one more week and then it will be time for baseball and here you are just getting started. Man, you're always slow!" I said I guessed everybody had his own way of doing things. He was pretty fast at doing things himself but he also lost his temper pretty fast and got into trouble. Henry might be a lot slower to make up his mind to do things but he did them pretty well after he got started. Earl turned to me to say, "Yeah, he's smart, I guess, because he did skip the third grade but he's slow doing anything. He don't want to do a lot of things 'til after we do them and then the next time, after we are all through, he wants to start them. He got left out of a lot of stuff that way last year." I said that was true, but certainly Henry wasn't getting left out of much this year and I was glad of that and so was he. . . .

A week later, Earl so lost control of himself in the group that the worker felt that the boy needed a chance to talk about it with him alone.

. . . As the boys piled into the car after the ball game, Earl accidentally stepped on Max, who retaliated by shoving Earl. At that, Earl completely lost his temper and started after Max with a rock he picked up from the road, shouting, "I'll kill that guy!" I got between them and Earl shouted, "You get out of the road, Mr. Ray. I'm going to split his head open!" I said that was exactly why I wouldn't get out of his way: I wasn't protecting Max—I was protecting him. Cliff said, "Cut it out, Early. You do that and you'll end up in jail, sure. Mr. Ray's only seeing you take care of yourself." Earl said that he wasn't fighting me. "I want that Max." I said that as long as he wanted to kill somebody, I guessed he'd be fighting me because I certainly wouldn't let him do that if I could help it. When Earl began to quiet down a little, I asked Max to get out of the car and rearranged the seating in the car. I told Earl to get in and cool off and that we could talk about this after the club meeting was over. . . .

When we arrived back at the agency, Earl and I talked about what had upset him and what he does to himself and others when he lets himself go. . . . He said, "Mr. Ray, I get so mad I can't see straight." I told him I knew that and could understand that he had a right to get mad but I was worried about what was going to happen to him. Earl leaned over, sort of putting his arms around my waist and said, "We're friends, aren't we, Mr. Ray?" And I responded, "You know we are, Earl. Even if you do something I don't like, you know I'm still your friend." He smiled a little wistfully and said, "You just tell Max to stay away from me, that's all!" I said I couldn't tell everybody in the world that he got mad at to stay away from him. Maybe he just had to learn to be with people and maybe be angry without getting so angry that he would mess up his life—and with that, he left.

In this three-week period of contact between worker and boy, the worker's efforts were concentrated on helping Earl in the various situations that arose in the group, attempting to hold him to an examination of his own feelings and responsibilities. He used the group's responses too, for the boys were jealous of their reputation as a club and clearly indicated by their comments that they were going to hold Earl to a certain degree of acceptable behavior while he was with them. When the boy gave in to uncontrolled impulse that was dangerous both to himself and to another member, the worker forcefully handled the immediate situation on the spot, but he knew that additional help was necessary and so he requested that they talk together after the rest of the group had left the agency.

The individual interview grew immediately out of the

group incident and the content of the interview centered around the boy's "mad" feelings in the group and his problem of controlling them. The worker could convey his understanding of these overpowering feelings that led him to loss of control, and he expressed even by words his concern for the boy. But far from taking the responsibility that Earl was hoping he would, he went on to put the responsibility for doing something about it squarely on Earl himself: "Maybe he just had to learn to be with people—" The worker couldn't protect him from everyone but by talking to him in this way, he could convey his belief that the boy could begin to find a way to control himself and to get along better with the other group members. Earl's only response was a wistful look, and the worker had to bear not knowing how much meaning this discussion had to him; only subsequent meetings would tell.

A boy who says, "I get so mad I can't see straight," may eventually need individualized help which the group work agency does not offer. The worker would need to be sensitive to that fact and act accordingly. But here the worker felt and conveyed his trust in the boy's ability to grow to use himself differently out of his experience with the group and the worker—and within the scope of the agency's function.

In what way does this kind of marginal interview contribute to fulfilling the agency's purpose? Is this part of the service to groups and its members? It was the boy's behavior in the group that precipitated the individual contact. The focus of the interview was on the boy's relation to other group members—a relationship which was full of frustration and confusion for the boy, and doubtless, of some sense of guilt. The worker revealed himself as a person concerned about the boy's difficulties with his fellow members and as one who expected that the boy could and would find a way to use himself differently. But this expectation is not on a personal level, for it is the agency's expectation that the worker offers to the boy. Miss Mazie Rappaport, out of her experience as administrator of a Protective Service for Girls, writes clearly on this point: "The amount of the agency expectation may be different for each client, for as the worker uses it, she relates always to the client's potential capacity to use himself. The agency by its expectation creates change in the client's situation—the change which comes from using a resource outside of himself to help him meet his problem. This has put something new into his way of meeting a problem, into his way of living. . . . The belief in the client's capacity rests on the purpose of the agency and the conviction that the client coming to a social agency has the right to responsible help, clearly offered, in which he has the choice of either doing something different about the way he meets his problem or of leaving this agency behind as offering something which he does not want or cannot use. Expectation thus provides the means by which the strength of the client can be discovered and affirmed by him." [6]

In the interview cited above, the worker does not explicitly present a choice to Earl in regard to his continuing use of the agency, although both the worker and the boy may have felt that to be implicitly between them. But the expectation is evident that this group member can find a different way for himself if he will.

Not only did the need for the interview arise from the group meetings, but it was understood by both of the persons engaged in the interview that it would be followed by other shared experiences in the group setting. The help given in the interview where the focus is on the member's group relations is continued in the group meeting where the worker is physically present as the member tests himself in a new way with his group.[7] The worker is there with his continuing support, expectation, and question— sometimes to be verbalized as the occasion demands but always to be felt by the member.

Turning to the interviews which are initiated by the group member, a variety of motivations may be assumed that impel the member to seek out the worker. It should be noted that rarely is an individual contact formalized by such a term as "interview" or "conference." Rather, it is known as a "talk," if it is labeled at all, and some of the most valuable results may come from the conversations that are not scheduled by appointment. The group member comes early to a meeting or lingers behind after the other members have gone; or he stops by the open door of the worker's office, in the hope that the worker will be free to talk to him. While some practical limits of time are necessary and helpful, the worker welcomes the member who moves out to him, no matter how tentatively or even negatively. Indeed, something of his interest in the member must have already been conveyed or he would not be sought out. The informality of the traditional group work agency with its frequent casual contacts between worker and members—in the hallway of the agency, on the street, or at the open door of the office—affords a positive service to agency members so long as the worker bears in mind that the person before him is an actual or potential agency group member.

The motivations for the self-initiated interview other than the familiar necessity to discuss program plans may be the wish for a closer relationship with the worker, a sense of some problem about other group members or himself as a group member, or a desire to talk over some personal problem of relationships that falls outside the agency experience. It is this latter area of problem that calls for an examination of its relation to agency function.

Some personal questions, such as vocational choices or pending induction into the armed services, may profitably be turned toward program possibilities for discussion in the group, in addition to pointing to specific resources for information on the subject and helping members to use such resources. But the more puzzling problems are those which have to do with personal family relationships that have produced deep emotional problems. What is the basis of the group worker's help to a group member who brings such problems to him? What direction for his help can he find in his agency's function? It is fruitless for the group worker to list problems and say, "These I will touch and these I will not." If the agency function is clearly in mind, the worker can test each situation against it. The basis for his help is not the problem which can be classified but the agency function.

THE REFERRAL PROCESS

When the worker is presented with a problem of relationships that lie outside the agency experience, he will try to find the connection between the personal problem and the member's relation to himself and the group. His responsibility does not necessarily end there, however. An important part of the group work agency's service is to work with members and their parents in a process of considering the use of other community services for help with problems that cannot be dealt with in the group work agency, possibly eventuating in a referral.

The process of referral comes about in one of two ways. Most commonly it is at the initiation of the worker whose experience with the group member indicates the need for specialized help. In cases in which the group work staff feels that a member is not able at the present time to use group experience, it is especially important to initiate with the member or his family the process of referral. Sometimes, after discussing the behavior of the member in the agency, it will suffice to name the available casework, medical, or psychiatric services and to give information about how such resources can be sought and used. More likely, however, members and their parents will need help in exploring their readiness to seek individual service and in considering what it may mean to them to become engaged with a casework agency or a therapist.

A second manner of moving into a referral process is in

response to the member or parent who comes asking for help with a family problem. The recorded experience of one group work agency, a neighborhood Center, will serve to point to the scope of the beginning phase of the referral process.

This is the case of Mr. and Mrs. Ward whose two daughters, Carol and Marie, were active in the Young Teen Division of the agency. At the beginning of the program year Carol had considerable difficulty in her club, but by the time of this recorded interview with her parents she had found a positive connection with the group and the agency. The parents, however, were troubled about her relation to them at home. In November, a group of parents of the Young Teen Division membership was called together by the agency for the purpose of discussing the parents' questions about the agency and interpreting the agency's objectives. This meeting was the first of a series in which parents and staff together discussed the nature of the young teen girl and her relationship to the adults in her life. It was through these meetings that Mrs. Ward developed a trust in the supervisor of the Division that led her to seek an interview with him and later to ask if she and her husband might both talk with him about their problems with their daughters. The interview took place immediately following a parents' meeting on February 15.

After the parents' meeting, Mr. and Mrs. Ward and I walked together to a vacant room. Mr. Ward looked a little bit frightened, as did his wife who said, smiling, "We're going to talk about Carol, aren't we?" We talked a little about some of the things the speaker, a psychiatrist, had just said in the meeting and when there was a pause, Mr. Ward asked me what this round-table discussion of ours was for. Mrs. Ward looked uncomfortable and I asked her husband what he had thought it was for. Mrs. Ward said that he knew very well why he was here. He responded to this immediately by saying that they have a problem in their family—that there is constant resentment and fighting between himself and his wife and he wants to do something about it. They agreed then that what they wanted to talk about was how they could begin to come to something consistent in their approach to their children. . . .

(Here the worker talked about Carol as he knew her in the agency and suggested that the good way she was now getting along in the agency must represent something positive in her life at home. This, Mrs. Ward denied, and both she and her husband gave examples of their different ways of approaching their daughters, disagreeing and resenting each other as they talked.)

For the most part I listened, making various comments to point up what they were saying. I finally said that what they were doing here in not being able to effect a compromise and discuss things together might be indicative of their family life. They both agreed that this was so. Mrs. Ward was angry at me because I was not giving them advice and telling her what to do. I told her what I *could* do to help them: to act as a resource to help them get to a place where they could work out these problems together.

I presented the possibilities of psychotherapy, marriage counseling, and casework at the Family Service. Mrs. Ward was quite against therapy because she felt it would be too nondirective. "They would just listen and not tell me what

to do." Both of them seemed the most interested in working with a marriage counselor.

I gave them some information on the Family Service in
regard to fees, the length of time before they might start
with the agency, suggesting some of the difficulties they
might face in continuing work with a caseworker, in their
own need to change, and how hard this might be. I told
them that I could help by making the initial contact but that
they would need to follow through with a call of their own.
Mrs. Ward was upset over the chance that the waiting period might extend ten months but recognized the fact that
the problem might still exist ten months from now. . . .

(There followed a recital of other troubling family inci-
dents which the worker had to interrupt.)

I attempted to summarize some of what they had been
saying and went on to ask them if they wanted me to call
Family Service as a starter, and then see them again to tell
them of the Family agency's response and to consider how
they themselves could proceed from there. Mr. Ward was
most amenable to this and happy that I was willing to take
the time. Mrs. Ward, too, responded affirmatively to my
question. When they started to get into further arguments
with each other, I said that I thought we could go no further. We could end here and I would be in contact with
them tomorrow after I had called Family Service. They left
expressing appreciation of the time I had spent with them.

Subsequent records reveal that six weeks later the
Wards were in direct contact with the Family Service.
The process for moving together toward casework service
was begun in their interview with the group worker. The
core of his help to them, within the function of his agency,

lay in helping them to choose an appropriate agency and to face what such a step might mean to them. His agency did not offer a marriage counseling service but it did provide a service that gave these parents some help in moving toward a community agency whose function is counseling.

When a person feels comfortable with his group worker and trusts him, it is quite natural to confide in him in the area of personal problems. If the worker is clear about his agency function, he will not be confused by these confidences. Wilson and Ryland write of this as follows: "[The group worker] uses his professional skill to understand the problems of the individual sufficiently to refer him to the appropriate agency, but he does not permit himself to become involved in helping the individual with his problems unless they are those which can be met within the service of groups. In all work with individuals the social group worker is guided by the knowledge of his specialized function in social work. The focus is that of enabling the individual to use the services of the group more effectively." [8]

The worker who encourages prolonged discussion of a member's personal problem quite apart from group relationships, and who moves into working on it with the member, will not only have moved away from the function of his agency but will have precipitated an intense, individual relationship with this group member which will interfere with the kind of help he could continue to give him in the group. The member, with self-consciousness and perhaps discomfort from having shared so much of his "out-of-the-group" self with the worker, or with a feeling of exclusive possessiveness of him, will be hampered in his freedom to develop relationships with the other group members.

Stability for both worker and member comes from the worker's sureness that his help lies primarily within the group process, with the conviction that as one is helped to a better and more responsible use of himself in group relations, he will find something that is his to use in other areas of relationship. It is not only that the group worker's competence lies within the group work process or that the group worker is "too busy" to devote time to working with members on their extra-group problems; either of these reasons would leave him full of guilt for what he cannot do for the person before him. The reason is a positive one—his function, given him and required of him by the agency's definition of its group work service. His direction as he works with individuals comes from that group work function, even as he acknowledges other areas of problem and helps the member to move into the same focus with him and the agency.

The definitive quality of agency function provides supporting limits both to the worker and to the group members if they are helped by the worker to comprehend and use them rather than to be confined by them. Who has not experienced the freeing quality of a limit? The child who plays happily in his large room only when he erects a semi-wall of toys and bookshelves to divide the space in half; the student who welcomes a clear-cut assignment of defined scope for a paper! An experience shared by many tourists in the mountainous regions of our country is to venture to the top of a fire tower where one is rewarded by a breath-taking panorama of mountains, trees, and valleys—overwhelming in its magnitude. But with the aid of the powerful lens of the forest ranger's telescope, the eyes can become focused on a distant mountain peak, with a clear and limited view of one particular spot. Thereafter, in relation to that one clearly defined point, the whole panorama is more comprehensible—the clouds above it, the ranges that extend in tiers below it. For the attention has been focused on a central point, temporarily eliminating the surrounding terrain.

In the difference between boundless, unlimited opportunity for activity, thought, and relationship and a known, definite focus, lies the difference between license and responsible freedom, between aimlessness and organized effort, between a sense of overwhelming pressures that immobilize and encompassable demands that stimulate deeper and forward movement.

The social agency function offers defined boundaries for giving and taking help that enhance the quality of the help so that deeper and more forward movement is possible. "Certainly function is never completely static or inflexible," wrote Dr. Jessie Taft, "certainly it alters over a period of time in terms of changing social conditions or should alter, but relatively, it is the known factor, the comparatively stable, fixed point about which client and worker may move without becoming lost in the movement." [9]

The skilled group worker comprehends and identifies

with the stable point of the agency—its function—with conviction that his work must be directed to helping people use the group experiences offered by the agency. Representing the agency rather than being disassociated from it, he offers agency group services, and using structures that provide choice to the group members, he helps them to move into the agency and, by making responsible choices, to use the part of the services in which they are ready to invest something of themselves and hence to use for their own growth.

Clarity about agency function, and ability to use it both for direction and selection of the worker's efforts and for a stable point from which process emanates, are essential to social group work skill. But skill does not rest alone on ability to use the agency function. Especially significant to the effective use of function are the worker's sensitivity to the feelings of the people with whom he works, and his ability to communicate with them. Without these qualities, the worker could be rigid and even punishing as he holds to agency function. We will turn next, then, to the aspect of group work skill that we shall call the ability to communicate on a feeling level, as such communication relates to fulfillment of group work purpose.

CHAPTER NOTES

1. See page 45.
2. Harleigh B. Trecker, *Social Group Work: Principles and Practices,* 2nd ed. (New York: Whiteside, 1955), pp. 30–31.
3. Again it should be noted that some multifunctional agencies (e.g., neighborhood houses), while loosely classified as group work agencies, often provide services in individual and family counseling, particularly in regard to referrals to other community resources.

In such cases, the intake worker would refer the applicant to the appropriate department and worker in his agency. See pages 84–88 for further discussion of referrals.

4. For the past several years group work agencies—settlements, national program organizations, and Jewish Centers—have been extending their services to include the leadership and organization of groups which meet on street-corners, at the neighborhood churches, temples, schools, or homes, rather than in the central buildings of the agencies.
5. Gertrude Wilson and Gladys Ryland, *Social Group Work Practice* (Boston: Houghton Mifflin, 1949), pp. 97–98, discuss the inevitable relatedness of the individual and the group.
6. Mazie Rappaport, "Casework with Adolescent, Delinquent Girls: the Dynamics of Expectation as a Psychological Concept in Working with Adolescent, Delinquent Girls," unpublished paper presented at the National Conference of Social Work, Atlantic City, April, 1948.
7. This structure for group work is a characteristic which distinguishes it from casework.
8. Wilson and Ryland, *op. cit.*, p. 75.
9. Jessie Taft, "The Relation of Function to Process in Social Case Work," *The Journal of Social Work Process,* I, 1937, p. 8.

CHAPTER IV

Skill in Communication of Feeling

THE SEARCH for satisfactory relatedness to others is a universal motivation for living. The factual, objective basis for relationships is the concrete, shared experience that consists of activities, decisions, agreements, and differences that are lived through together by two or more persons. To consider these concrete contacts the whole of relationship, however, is to deny the inevitability and importance of the feeling that flows between people as they are in contact with each other. For in every human relationship are emotional reactions to one's self, to the other person, and to the specific content of the mutual experience.

"There can be no relationship without . . . alive and responsible evidences of a self which are involved in the expression of feeling." [1] Not only is feeling present, but also it must be expressed if there is to be communication, synonymously described as "connection" between people.

In this chapter we are concerned with the questions of

what is meant by the communication of feelings in the group work process; what is required of the worker if he is to develop helpful feeling relationships with his group members; and finally, how the skill of communication effects movement toward the group work purpose of developing responsible behavior.

THE WORKER'S FEELINGS

High among the qualities essential to a social worker's skill is the capacity to feel with others. Perhaps the most commonly expressed motivation for entering the profession of social work is concern for people and their welfare. But this very quality of concern for others can be translated into helping only if it is acknowledged and disciplined so that it does not control the worker in his relationships with those whom he would help, and so that he is free to sense and meet the feelings that are theirs and distinct from his own. "The social work student needs to learn how to deal with his own natural response to human need, despair and difference, often grotesque and extreme, in ways that are conducive to establishing a vital helping relationship to the individual or group. He needs to learn, too, the masks and disguises the human self takes when it has lost its way or is pushed to the limit of its endurance and to respond accurately and immediately to the feeling tone rather than to the shocking behavior. Old lay attitudes, suitable or appropriate for one's personal code of conduct, need to give way to compassion as a component of professional understanding." [2]

In order to discipline his feelings that they may be

available for professional use, the worker must acknowledge their presence. Feeling is two-sided; rarely does one experience "pure" feeling—all negative or all positive. Rather there is a combination of the two, shifting back and forth as one part of the self finds something good and exciting and another part of the self finds it fearful and hard to bear—part wanting, and part not wanting. To deny either part of the feeling is to deny reality; and so the worker, if he is to use his feelings constructively in relationship with his group members, must constantly face, acknowledge, and claim the feelings that are his. The worker who can admit to himself that he has some of the apprehension over meeting a new group that is universal to approaching new and unfamiliar experiences in which one has an investment, has made a start toward dissipating that fear and organizing his strengths to meet the situation, to an extent that would not have been possible had he let himself feel only the positive anticipation of the experience. Or the worker who controllingly and willfully presents and promotes a program of activities because he so much wants to have a "successful" group has to realize that he is operating from his insecurity and his need to prove himself adequate, before he can let go of his high-handed control and be free to engage the group members in the development of their group activities.

Rather than face one's painful, unpleasant feelings, it is tempting to try to make someone else carry the responsibility and blame for them, to project them on another person. The beginning worker, for example, may encounter difficulty in presenting and holding to necessary limits as he works with his group, believing that the members dislike any kind of limits and prefer license in what they do. If the worker can face the fact that he himself has not come to terms with authority, he can take back his projection and can begin to understand that the members of his group are actually seeking in him the strength that will set some supporting boundaries to their behavior.

The denial of feeling may err on the positive side as well as the negative. For the worker must be able to affirm his strengths, not only admit to his problems, if he is to have something positive to bring to his groups. Such feelings as confidence in one's self and warm acceptance of others must be recognized as real if they are to be conveyed to others.

While words express feeling, they are not the only means of communication. It is often the facial expression, the gesture, the air of the person, that carries the emotion to be sensed undeniably and received by another. The artist who himself has experienced deep feeling knows this well, since his medium does not include verbal or written expression in words. Several years ago the artist, James Chapin, created a fine lithograph which he entitled "Communication." [3] He has caught and portrayed a precious moment of deep understanding between a mother and her young child as they gaze at each other. It is a moment of relatedness conveyed through the facial expression and posture of the two figures.

In the group work process it is the worker's responsibility to initiate the process of communication; and therein lies the legitimacy for his concern with his own feeling, that it may free him to be sensitive to what his group members are feeling and really to hear what they are saying by their words and actions—in short, to establish communication with them. But for the worker to be aware of his feeling is not enough; he has to let the members experience a real part of it. Whether it is positive or negative, the members have the right to know it as something real to be responded to. For many years students at the University of Pennsylvania School of Social Work have been helped to this realization by an early paper of Dr. Jessie Taft's in which she addressed herself to the process of growth through feeling relationships between children and adults. She wrote: "Emotion responds only to emotion; the self goes out and expands only in the presence of a respect and acceptance which he can feel. The child has a right to experience not only his own feelings but the emotional reactions which he arouses in the parents, to feel his own power over them as well as theirs over him, to know their momentary hates, fears and rages, as well as their supporting love and tenderness. . . ." [4]

The worker's focus as he expresses feeling, then, cannot be on his own need to be spontaneous, but must be centered on the group members' need to know and experience the reality of genuine emotion from another, if they, with the worker, are to create something valid for themselves through their group participation. The professional nature of the relationship between worker and members demands, however, that the worker discipline the expression of his feeling if it is not to damage the group. This means that the worker must find for himself a balance between spontaneity and discipline—between freedom and control.

There is a unique kind of demand for a combination of spontaneity and control in the very nature of the group worker's participation in his relations with his groups. A large proportion of the worker's time with groups in leisure-time agencies is spent in informal activities—games, camping, dancing, eating, for example—in all of which the worker participates as part of his worker responsibility. If he is to help his members to benefit from these activities, he must himself get some satisfaction from them, or at least have appreciation and some feeling for the creative enjoyment that is possible as one participates in recreational activities. He has to have some enthusiasm for them, stemming from his own experience or from his willingness to find out what they are like. The familiar caricature of one who works with groups in informal activities is as a hearty, enthusiastic person who is constantly and jovially urging into lively activity any group of people whom he encounters. Distressing as such a picture is to a group worker, there is undeniably more than a grain of truth in the implication that the group worker must possess an outgoing quality as part of his personality. The worker who finds himself uncomfortable and reticent with groups finds it difficult indeed to help others relate to groups. There has to be something in him that is ready to move out to a group of people, although with the sensitivity that will help him to avoid projecting his warmth so forcibly that it will feel overwhelming to the others, or block them in their responses.

To use one's outgoingness helpfully, requires conscious discipline of impulse. For while the group worker may find himself quite comfortable with a group, and while he may have genuine pleasure in the activities he is helping the group members to use, he is with the group as a worker whose function is to help its members use the group experience for their social development. And so he must contain the two sides within himself—the spontaneous, outgoing quality, and the disciplined, controlled consciousness of how he is using himself in relation to his groups. If his primary concern is for the feelings of his group members and the freeing of them for responsible use that can lead to their relatedness to him and to fellow members, he discovers an inevitable control on a licensed expression of his own emotions. He is with the group to help it and his consciousness of that fact gives direction to responsible communication of the feeling part of himself in a genuine though disciplined way.

The Group Members' Feelings

We have been speaking of the worker's awareness, expression, and discipline of his feelings as they affect his readiness to sense and respond to the feelings of the members of his groups, and contribute to his creative use of himself in relationships. We turn now to question how the worker can help the members to know, accept, express, and be responsible for *their* feelings. Sensitivity to the group's feeling is not enough, although it is an important step in relationships. Neither is response to members' feelings helpful unless it is directed toward encouraging the members to own them and be responsible for them.

The shades of feeling of the members of any one group at any given meeting are myriad, and may range from extreme positiveness to extreme hostility. The positive feelings are less likely to be expressed verbally, as compared with the troublesome ones, since there is a tendency to take the "good" feelings for granted. It is important for the worker to help the members to identify the positive parts of their experiences together for what they may carry of a sense of growth and self-affirmation, to be used to build on in subsequent experiences. Take, for example, the satisfaction over the completion of some program project in which the members have invested a great deal of themselves; the exhilaration of liking each other and doing things together, of sharing mutual problems; the creative use of program media; the positive sense of being part of a whole—the group, the agency, the community. The worker's recognition of these positive emotions, and encouragement to the members to put some of their feelings into words, help them to affirm their shared experience and to move ahead together as a group.

No matter how positive and real the feelings may be at any given moment, and no matter how sensitively the worker acknowledges and responds to them, he must be equally concerned with the part of the feeling that even then is negative or that may emerge at the very next moment. When negative feelings are overtly expressed in

violent words or in disruptive behavior, the worker has
little choice as to whether or not he will sense or respond
to the feeling, for the very demands of the members' behavior force him to deal with it. In content, negativeness
comes out around agency policies or structures, in personal antagonisms between members, frustrations over
program, in fears related to moving out to new contacts
and experiences, or in hostility against the worker himself. But the feeling produced by such circumstances is not
always readily expressed by words or aggressive behavior,
but may be conveyed by withdrawal or by apparent in-
difference to the group's affairs or to the worker. It is a
temptation to the worker, not wanting to hear and face
the unpleasant, to disregard the unexpressed feelings—indeed, to attempt to deny their existence—in an effort to
move the group ahead positively in feeling and action, although falsely and unrealistically based.

Illumination of what it can mean to a group when the
worker acknowledges prevailing negative feelings is afforded by the following record of an experienced social
group worker who, as part of the Social Service Department
of a State Mental Hospital, is assigned to the Pre-Parole
Service for patients.[5] The eight men comprising the group,
all from the Epileptic Colony of the hospital, had met
for a time or two with a worker who unexpectedly left the
employ of the hospital at that point. Following the de-
parture of their worker, they had one session with the director of the Social Service Department, and then started
again with the group worker who was assigned to help
them in eight sessions to explore their readiness to move

out of the hospital, and to give them a chance to make responsible choices as evidence of their increasing ability to face reality as they move toward possible parole. The first step was for each one to decide if he wanted to use this group service the hospital was offering; but the worker knew that he must start with helping them all express and own whatever problem they were feeling about the rapid succession of workers assigned to them.

Most of the patients arrived in the meeting-room by ten minutes before ten, and there was a good deal of lively kidding about many things—women patients who could be seen through the window, smoking, distorting last names, etc.—all of which seemed to me to be a cover-up for some of the fears and anxieties they had in coming to this new worker and a comparatively new situation. Much of this was stimulated by the two younger members, Mr. Henry and Mr. Powell. I participated in some of this small-talk and joking, being careful at the same time to maintain my difference. Soon, Mr. Henry told me that all he needed was work, and that was his big problem. I knew they were anxious to begin the meeting, but wondered if we could wait until the set time, to give all the members a chance to arrive. Meantime, we might use the time to get acquainted with each other's names. They agreed and each, in turn, told me his name. I repeated each of the last names, with the title of Mister. (Everyone in the Colony from which they come calls them by first names.) When Mr. Powell's turn came, he hesitated, started to say "Carl," and then with much pride gave his name as "Mr. Powell." It seemed that every man's chest expanded at this.

By now it was ten o'clock, and I suggested we begin. Mr.

Henry wondered whether I knew everybody's name now. I recognized this as testing and said I would try, and went around the circle, repeating each name. I might make mistakes in the future, but I was trying hard now because I felt that each one of them was an individual and important to me as such, and each of them had certain rights which I would try to respect as we went along. They wanted me to spell my name, which I did, and now Mr. Powell showed his card with my name misspelled and said he was glad he had it right now.

This led to my saying seriously that maybe some of them were glad that I was finally here, and some were not. I did want them to know that I could understand that they might be a little impatient with Social Service, since I was the third worker to start with their group—and a little mad, too. Mr. Ames quickly corrected me, saying that the word was "angry" and all laughed. I said, "Yes, angry too, and maybe a little fearful, or perhaps so disgusted already that you won't even be able to work with me." About all I could say was that they had a right to feel abandoned and impatient.

At this point, Mr. Henry said that he didn't have any feelings about all that had been happening—only he was a little impatient at the time it was taking for him to get out of the hospital. Mr. Powell said that he always has a smile on his face, and he'll smile at and with me, too. Mr. Stone denied any feelings of hurt, and he indicated that he would take help however and whenever it was given. Before I could say anything, a little friendly group interplay took place, and in this came all the hurt, impatience, and fear that I might not be around long either. They said it seemed to take forever to get anywhere with Social Service. Soon this became a direct outpouring of hostile feelings against me, and all the pent-up hurt came out. Now the group felt a little guilty for this, and they were thus amazed when I told them I was glad they could share this with me, that they had a right to these feelings, and that I was truly sorry they had to go through all this. The thing was that now I was here offering this service, and what, if anything, could they do with it? I had every intention of seeing them through this, if they wished. Mr. Stone said I didn't look like the kind of person who would let them down. I couldn't guarantee that I would be here, and Mr. Dawes, in a limited way, told them that people get sick and die. All I could say was that I would try very hard to be with them. As to time, I could only tell them that the most I could give them would be eight weeks. Mr. Henry asked if it couldn't be done sooner —getting ready to leave the hospital—and I said yes, that it certainly could, and it depended on each one; some would be faster and some slower. Having been hurt, could they bear to go on, make a new start? For I was here now, and what did they want to do with it?

Now came a heart-warming affirmation of wanting to see what they could do with what was left for them, of trust that there was something, and that they wanted to "try" me and see. Dramatically, Mr. Powell pulled down a window-shade to block off the men's view of the women patients who had distracted them, and this seemed to be their way of saying to me, "Let's begin and we mean business!"

I told them why they had been referred to this group, and we examined the choices they had now of the various ways of leaving the hospital. When we talked of elopement (leaving the hospital without authorization), Mr. Powell expressed the group's point of view that you would be brought back only if you left on your own; you had to live with yourself, so why not leave the right way? Each man in turn told of his particular circumstances, the job he was doing here in the hospital, etc., and most of them seemed to be moving toward Foster Care. I held them to not deciding today whether they could use the Pre-Parole service and go on with me, though each person seemed to have about decided to do so.

There was a great deal of movement and understanding that amazed me when I told them some of the requirements for using this service. They said they thought they could go somewhere with me. I was glad they could feel this way, but I knew that everything wasn't all rosy for I had a real "show me" attitude of what they could do here in the hospital, and they might rightfully have some resentment about it. They would let me know when they did! They will be meeting with me on Fridays at ten o'clock.

Now, as the time was up, each man came and shook hands with me. I was moved when Mr. Stone, unashamedly, kissed my hand and said it was for luck and because I was here. Before the men left, I told them all that I was aware of their real strength in being able to decide to use these meetings as a way of beginning to move out of the hospital, and the men seemed to be pretty proud of themselves.

In many respects, the work presented by this record represents skillful practice. The worker's efforts are directed, by the function of his department, to helping the patients find a connection with social reality—the reality here being the structure of a series of meetings in which, step by step, they can discover and test their readiness to move out into the community, away from the protection of the institution. With the conviction that these patients have the strength, if they can organize it, to make responsible choices with self-determination, he engages them in a process with him in which he makes it clear that theirs is the responsibility to determine their future in the way they plan for it. He cannot plan for them, but he will be there to help them. But he knows that they cannot be free to move forward if they are holding pent-up feelings of hostility or despair, so he enables them to face their troubled feelings, to admit to these feelings to the point of expressing and discussing them. His welcoming response assured them that here and with him they could be "real," and they were freed by this assurance to move ahead to the positive though partial decision that they would like to "try" working with him. Regardless of how much he hoped these men could achieve parole status, he had to be attuned to the reality of their feelings at the very moment he was with them, if he was to free them for responsible movement.

Of the quality of his own feeling, the worker conveyed to the group his concern for them as individual persons whose feelings and opinions he valued and respected as he expressed his willingness to meet with them, his understanding of their doubts and fears, and his acceptance of their feelings, both bad and good. The developing relationship between them stemmed from the worker's freedom to connect with their feelings aroused by the social realities of the current hospital experience, the specific service, and the professional self he was offering them. Indeed, it was his clarity about his own and his agency's aim

to help patients take steps toward responsible relationships, combined with his ability to convey feeling and to
enable them to do so, that produced the helpful quality
of his work.

In the process of helping people become more responsible for their behavior, one must often carry the difficult
task of facing the group member with reality that arouses
feelings most painful for him to bear. Sensitivity to these
feelings, but willingness to let the other person have them,
are essential if the worker is to communicate with the
group member.

A poignant example of sensitive relatedness, while
facing a member with the reality of the effect of his behavior on the group, is to be found in the following account of an interview between a student-worker and a
fourteen-year-old boy, Charlie, who wanted to join the
Hawks, a club in a Jewish Center. According to the membership practices of the club, a majority of its members
had to favor the admission of a new member. When
Charlie's name first came up for consideration, there was
a lot of question about him as a desirable member, and
violent criticism of him as a boy who talks too much and
always wants to have his own way. With the worker's help,
the boys decided to invite him to attend two trial meetings, after which they would decide about his admission.
The worker talked to Charlie, telling him of the questions the other boys had raised, and Charlie decided to
attend the two probationary meetings. When the time
came, in Charlie's absence, to vote on his application for
membership, none of the boys voted for him, although

some abstained from voting. Later in the evening, the worker found him in the game-room and told him of the club's decision.

> . . . Charlie said he wanted to know one thing: would I tell him how many boys voted against his being in the club? I tried to say that it wasn't really important, but Charlie said that it was important to him. I told him that two fellows had voted not to have him in the club. He said, "See? Only two fellows are against me!" I felt very badly, knowing that Charlie must know he was not wanted unconditionally by any of the boys. I said, "Charlie, no fellow voted to have you as a member—only as a guest." He said, "No one?" and I said, "No." He was quiet and tears welled in his eyes. I felt like a brutal person. I put my arm around him and said, "Charlie, I told you this because I wanted you to know the truth. I know it's hard, but if you think it is just a few of the boys who don't want you in the club, then you will think it isn't *you,* and you will go on just as you always have, losing friends instead of making them."
>
> I just sat there with my arm on his while he wiped his eyes. I asked what he was thinking about. "Of my filibustering and wanting my own way." I said it was good that we knew two things we could work on. He wiped his eyes again and said, "Yes, but that not wanting my own way— that's going to be tough! . . ."[6]

There was fine relatedness between these two, worker and group member, as they talked so earnestly about the boy's relationship to his peers. The worker sensed deeply this young boy's disappointment, but he felt, too, his need and desire to do something different about himself. He was torn, but only for a moment, between his compassion, which tempted him to protect the boy from the truth, and his deeper, still compassionate concern as a helper, which led him to helping the boy face the reality of his own part in relationships. If he had revealed the truth without feeling and conveying his concern, he would have been punishing—"brutal," as he said. The worker let the boy experience the two balancing sides of his feeling: the warmth of the helper who cares about his disappointment, but who cares deeply enough to hold him to facing his own responsible part in his relationships with other boys he wants as friends. This was feeling available for use in the service of another.

With this connection as a basis for working together, the boy would know that he could count on the agency's continuing help. The worker had said to him, "It is good that we know two things *we* can work on," indicating that he or other agency workers would help him in his relationship to other boys, perhaps in a loosely organized group, such as in a game-room, or eventually in a club group. If his difficulty in social relationships proved serious enough, it is likely that his parents would become engaged with the agency in considering the services of another agency. The worker here conveyed his expectation that the boy could change his part in social relations, and his assurance that he would not have to struggle with it all by himself.

GROUP FEELING

In the instance just cited, the worker was dealing with the feelings of one potential group member, separated from the others as they discussed his relations with them. But in the usual group work situation, when several members are together, the worker faces a complexity of feelings. He confronts the separate and individual reactions of as many persons as there are members present; each member's feeling may be like, or quite different from, those of his fellow members. The interaction of each member to the others and to the worker produces something new—a group feeling. It is false, however, to conceive of group feeling as simply the composite of the distinct feelings of a number of people, for the presence of each person with his particular attitudes contributes to the whole, and changes the character of it. As Muller writes: ". . . the whole organism is not a mere aggregate but an architecture; . . . Although parts and processes may be isolated for analytical purposes, they cannot be understood without reference to the dynamic, unified whole that is more than their sum." [7]

Group feeling, more than the sum of the feelings of all of the group members, is a somewhat intangible quality but clearly identifiable to one who is free to sense it. It is the tone, the spirit, the air, that permeates a group—be it anticipation, fear, excitement, suspicion, hostility, determination. Group work language is confusing in the dual meaning given to the term "group feeling." Sometimes it is used to describe group cohesion and unity, a oneness of feeling that stems from the members' strong identification with the group. But in a broader sense, the term connotes whatever is the predominant feeling of the group as a whole, which may well include group identification or, at the other extreme, a sense of disorganization or scatter; and it is in this wider sense that we are here using the term.

Group psychologists for many years have given their attention to the phenomenon of group behavior, and have sought to identify the factors that contribute to certain kinds of group feeling that lead to group behavior patterns.[8] Among these writers, Dr. Redl, in two recently published books, has described and analyzed the individual and group behavior of emotionally disturbed children in an experimental "group therapy" home.[9] He uses the phrase "group psychological intoxication" to describe the undisciplined feelings that frequently spread from one child to the others, resulting in wild and irresponsible behavior of most of the group. "Beginning with some minor, free-floating contagion of the one or the other more excited youngster, the whole group sometimes may break out into stages of impulsive wildness which surpass anything that we usually would expect of it. Such a 'group mood' seems to be especially catching." [10]

This kind of contagion of mood is not unfamiliar to the worker in the traditional group work agency that primarily serves people who are not deeply disturbed emotionally, as were the children described by Dr. Redl. Positive moods, too, are catching. Quick changes are possible, so that in the short span of a few minutes the group feeling may shift from the steadiness that accompanies a cooperative, shared experience in which all members are interested, to the sudden emergence of a disorganized kind of excitement in which each member pits himself against the others or against the worker, or may turn from hostility and impatience to a calmer, more positive mood. Whatever the group feeling, the worker must be attuned to it and recognize it as real.

It is not always possible to know what produces the group's predominant feeling of the day; the elusive quality of the mood of any particular moment often cannot be explained. This quality may be due to the feelings and resulting behavior of individual members, especially those whose status in the group is high; or to events and experiences between meetings; or to the worker's and agency's expectation of them which calls forth an immediate feeling response. The worker can help them to understand why they are feeling as they are, and to acknowledge their feelings and take some responsibility for them, as a means of enabling them to move toward the goal of increasing self-responsibility.

Part of the worker's skill lies in his effectiveness in introducing his difference of feeling and idea that the members can respond to, as he keeps himself free to be related to their emotions, attitudes, and ideas. This constant connection with the group requires letting go of some attitudes valued by the worker, shifting and yielding at points. It does not permit the worker to hold doggedly to what he determines as "best for the group," even though he tries to soften his control and ease his guilt by engaging with his members in something like a Socratic dialogue, while still intent on gaining his point. In such an instance he would still be operating from his own manipulative feeling, however benign in quality. Group members are quick to sense the difference between the worker who attempts to impose his feelings on them (to which overt resistance is the usual response), and the one who helps them to modify their feelings by honestly expressing his own as different and helping them to understand and claim theirs as real.

But the worker's question as to precisely when to hold to his original feeling and judgment, and when to go along with the group, is a puzzling one, unless the worker has available for his use a clear and strong connection with his group members. Admittedly, in the process of working with any group, many factors, both concrete and fundamental, call for firm holding on the part of the worker. Insistence on process, conviction in the right of every member to be heard, certain agency policies—these the worker must stand on firmly. But the skillful worker, even as he holds to such stable parts of his help, can yield to the members' difference, to their own pace in coming to shifts of feeling, to their aggression and withdrawal at spots. He must be free enough to let his group members have their feelings and to act on them, even to the point of coming to a decision quite different from one that, to him, seems more advantageous for them.

As one examines the nature of the group work process, it seems clear that a major determinant of its effectiveness lies in the worker's ability to connect with the feeling of his group members, to the end of helping them own and use their feelings responsibly in relationships. The relatedness sought by the worker develops as he engages with the members in the reality that encompasses both the concrete aspects of agency function, group activities, and decision, and the feelings that surround such specificity. The reality provides the structure for developing relationships. When the worker, disciplined to distinguish his own emotional reaction from that of the members, can be free to comprehend and respond to the feelings of others, he has discovered a skill essential to helping the members of his groups in their movement toward social growth.

CHAPTER NOTES

1. Frederick H. Allen, *Psychotherapy with Children* (New York: Norton, 1942), p. 260.
2. Faculty, University of Pennsylvania School of Social Work, unpublished report, 1955.
3. James Chapin, "Communication," lithograph printed by Associated American Artists (New York).
4. Jessie Taft, "Living and Feeling," *Child Study*, X, January, 1933, p. 109.
5. This is defined by the hospital manual as "a casework service available upon medical referral to all patients who are considered by their doctor to be ready to begin planning for the future. The service is offered to all who are referred, and is given to those who want help in exploring the possibilities open to them through a series of interviews or group meetings. It is a time-limited experience in relationship with a professional caseworker that requires the patient to assume a growing responsibility for himself in his present situation and for each decision and choice made along the way in his own planning for his immediate future." (The work presented here is that of a group worker.)
6. George Brager, "Group Autonomy and Agency Intake Practice," *Group Work and Community Organization*, 1953–54 (New York:

Columbia University Press, published for the National Conference of Social Work, 1954), p. 9. In this paper Mr. Brager sharply and forthrightly questions agency membership practices that tend to produce such painful experiences for its members.

7. Herbert J. Muller, *Science and Criticism* (New Haven: Yale University Press, 1936), p. 107, quoted in Sinnott, *Cell and Psyche: the Biology of Purpose,* p. 21.
8. For example, Kurt Lewin, Ronald Lippitt, Theodore Newcomb, Fritz Redl.
9. Fritz Redl and David Wineman, *Children Who Hate* (Glencoe, Ill.: Free Press, 1951); and Fritz Redl and David Wineman, *Controls from Within* (Glencoe, Ill.: Free Press, 1952).
10. Redl and Wineman, *Children Who Hate,* p. 89.

CHAPTER V

Skill in Using the Reality of the Present

WE HAVE BEEN SPEAKING of the reality inherent in the concreteness of agency function and in the feelings held by group members as they use what the agency has to offer through its worker. Both by implication and explicit statement the idea has been forwarded that engagement in the group work process takes place in a current moment of time shared by worker and group members. What is the significance of the present in time? What are the dynamic possibilities for individual and group movement toward group work purpose in the actual and current moments of a group meeting? Most pertinent to our inquiry: What is the nature of the worker's skill that enables him, with sureness and helpfulness, to use the present for significant movement of the group? These are the questions to be explored in the pages that follow, starting with the examination of two illustrative pieces of recorded group work practice for its identifiable skill and evidences

116

of its contribution toward achievement of professional purpose.

UTILIZING THE GROUP'S CURRENT INTEREST FOR PURPOSEFUL ACTIVITY

The first piece of material has been selected deliberately because of the age of the group members, from sixty to eighty-seven—an age in which it is especially important and sometimes difficult to find satisfaction in the present. Each time a student-worker takes on for the first time the leadership of an older adult group, he has to work through his initial feeling that his group members are too old to change their pattern of relationships or to take increasing responsibility for their lives; that their lives are behind them, and that the present can have little meaning for them except as preparation for the end of life. The impact of the group itself changes the attitude and expectation of the worker who lets himself feel the vitality of the members. Thus one student-worker wrote: "At first I felt that older adults had finished growing, that they had reached a point at which change and growth were no longer possible. . . . But in the process of working with this group, I discovered the real strength that people possess and the growth that can take place, despite physical weakness and deterioration of bodies. . . . It suddenly burst upon me like a revelation that the relationships within the group, their talk of love affairs, their preoccupation with life and living, were all evidence that these people were very much alive and involved in the present." [1] With realization and expectation that older adults are both able and eager to take a dynamic part in their current group life, the worker can help them to value and find a responsible place for themselves as they work together on some of their current problems of living. The following record illustrates this.

The "Old Cronies" are all men—men of a variety of races and nationalities, most of them widowers or bachelors who live alone in cheap rooming houses and who are recipients of some form of public assistance. Their club, the Old Cronies, was organized by workers of an interracial settlement house where they met weekly for an entire afternoon. While the club had been in existence for several years, it had been assigned to a new worker only two months prior to the meeting recorded here. Just before Thanksgiving the club, considering whether they might contribute cans of food to an agency project, moved into a discussion of some of the practices of the visitors from the City Department of Public Assistance, as they had known or heard about them:

... Mr. Reidner said, "Don't get caught with an extra can of food if you don't want to get cut." Mr. Franklin added that he was right and Mr. Reidner continued to storm. His comments were affirmed and added to by several others and everyone became very excited. They spoke in high voices and were fiery in manner. I permitted this to go on for a time as they exchanged stories. At the end of one of Mr. Randall's stories, I quietly asked, "What have you done about all this?" Then came a barrage of: "What the hell can you do about it?" and indictments of everyone from Eisenhower to the local visitor.

What I gathered from their stories was that they felt that
families in similar circumstances were treated differently
according to their particular visitor. I asked what they
thought they might do about it if they wanted to do something. "They ought to be hanged. We ought to make them
try to live on what they give us." I asked, "What would
either of those ideas benefit you?" There was a moment of
quiet, then of rumbling, until Mr. Reidner lashed out again
with, "They ought to be reported!" I wondered who should
be reported but he wasn't sure except that it was the ones
who make the budget cuts. "Who makes the cuts?" I asked.
There was confusion. Some thought the visitor; others, the
politicians in City Hall or in Harrisburg or "all the way
up" in Washington. I wondered if there was any way of
finding out what was going on, what the real story was, who
made the cuts and why. Mr. Reidner said we should get a
newspaper reporter down here and tell him the story—then
we would see what happens! I said that would be one way
but was anyone sure of his particular case and the facts surrounding it? No one was sure but all felt something was
wrong. I asked how they could challenge anything if they
didn't know the law governing the grants. Maybe what was
happening was legitimate. Was there any advantage in dealing with this problem as a group? They mentioned a lot of
reasons why they thought this was a good idea.

I asked how many thought the club, all of them together,
might do something about the situation. They raised their
hands and expressed agreement. Mr. Reidner said he could
bring in fifty people to testify. Others estimated how many
they could bring. The discussion was starting to get out of
focus and I said in a louder voice than before, "O.K., you
fellows have voiced your disapproval of what has been hap-

pening and you want to do something about it as a group. Now you aren't sure of the facts of the law and we ought to be able to get those facts some way." Mr. King asked, "How are you going to do that? Are *you* going to read the law?" I said I wasn't an expert in this but I thought the Department of Public Assistance had experts on the subject who could tell us what we wanted to know. Mr. Randall wanted to know who was going to ask them. I wondered if the club might ask them about it. Mr. Lewis thought they wouldn't listen to any of them—they would just laugh at them. Then they told me about last year when they had invited a speaker from the Department of Public Assistance and it had just been a farce.

I said that might all be true but that I knew of no way to do anything about the questions that were troubling them until they had the facts. Mr. Franklin asked what would happen after they got the facts, and Mr. Reidner said, "Then we ought to prosecute someone!" It seemed to me that if there were infractions of the laws, each case would have to be handled on an individual basis. It was Mr. Rutherford who pointed out that sometimes the laws were no good and Mr. O'Reilly, speaking for the first time asked, "What happens then?"

I asked how laws are changed if they need to be or how laws are made in the first place. Three or four of the men tore apart all of the politicians they could think of and Mr. Rush told how he had "played ball" with one of the local politicians who had promised him everything but had come through with nothing. This was confirmed by several others and I thought maybe they would think twice next time. Mr. Young stood up then and told the group that elections had been held recently and there were new people in the state legislature where Public Assistance laws were made and they were the people who could change the grants. He told about the Townsend club of which he is president and what they are trying to do about legislation. I asked him to describe how they got started on legislative programs and added some explanation of my own as to the possibilities of expressing themselves to legislators.

Now I summarized the ideas that had come out in this meeting and asked if they wanted to invite someone from the Department of Public Assistance to talk with them. All agreed they did, so I asked how we would go about getting a speaker here. Mr. Franklin suggested writing a letter and when I asked who would write it, Mr. Reidner suggested the Neighborhood House. I said that was a possibility but was the agency staff the group that really wanted to know? He replied with, "You write the letter and I'll sign it. I don't care; they don't scare me." I asked him if he would be willing to help me compose a letter and he said he would; but when I asked who else would help, there was silence. Finally I said, "The letter doesn't have to be signed by individual members but by the whole club. What we need is another person or two to help put down the facts and questions as the club sees them." This brought the services of Mr. King and Mr. Randall.

Mr. Franklin said that he would bring his wife to the meeting and others chimed in, saying they would bring "a whole pack of people to show them that we have force." I asked them to think what that would be like. Were we sincerely interested in getting information or were we inviting a visitor here to "put him on the hot seat"? Mr. Young said, "That's right. Let's not make a big stink when we don't know what we are doing yet. Let's get this guy down here and take down what he says!" When I asked again how this sounded to the rest of them, they all agreed except Mr. Reidner who still wanted someone from the press at the meeting. They all looked at me and I suggested that in line with Mr. Reidner's remarks, we wait until we know where we are going and first find out the facts. They voiced approval of this approach.

I reviewed their plan of action and, at the end, suggested that this might lead to something or nothing for them. Mr. Franklin ended the discussion with "Well, we got nothing to lose." They all agreed and Mr. King remarked, "Now we're going! This was a good discussion!" I told the group of letter writers that I would meet with them during the refreshment period to compose the letter with them. . . .

Only a worker who held as a basic value the belief that these aged men had strength to act for themselves and capacity to grow through current relationships with each other and him could have held them so consistently to participation in the process of responsible planning. His was an active part in the meeting. Accepting their projections, their expressions of frustration and hostility, he constantly brought them to the question of what they themselves could do "right here and now" about their common problem with their Public Assistance grants— both the actual amount of the grants and their feelings about them. Primarily, the men were expressing their frustration over the system they felt caught in and they were blaming everyone connected with Public Assistance for their situation. The worker was sensitive to this feel-

ing, listening to their complaints; but he pulled their attention directly back to the present and to their own
strength and responsibility as a group, when he asked,
"What can you do about it?" He focused on their responsibility for exploring the facts of the situation and helped
them consider concrete ways of learning the facts they
needed. More than that, he conveyed his expectation that
it was they who would take responsible steps in pursuing
their interest and that he could not do it for them. He
was not caught in trying to make things right for them,
for example, by looking up the Welfare laws and reporting to them, or writing letters for them, for he knew that
they must be involved in action themselves if the experience was to have any meaning for them. And yet, his expectation did not exceed what they were capable of doing,
as he offered his help on each of these steps and helped
the men consider their request for a speaker as a group
project that would not threaten any of its members.

While the discussion encompassed both the past experiences of the men and something of their future goals
and hopes, it was concentrated primarily, by the worker's
questions, on what they could do in association with each
other in their club meetings. Every member had the
chance to be part of the process of expressing opinions,
considering those of others, deciding on first steps of action. All came to the realization that they were doing
something about their dissatisfaction, that they were moving away from the frustrating block of the past; and all
this, in relation to each other and the worker. While they
were inclined to think that the virtue of their strength

lay in the size and united-front quality of their club, they were actually experiencing the sort of yielding and affirming that accompanies a group decision as they responded to the difference, the question, and the focus that their worker introduced. For the worker held them to mature opinions and actions, suggesting that they take their complaints directly where they belonged, not to each other or to him, and that they plan their meeting, not as a protest, but as a means of gaining knowledge of facts. This course called for honest facing of their attitudes and considerable change. It is understandable that at the end of the meeting, one member could say, "This was a good discussion!"—for by an interacting process between members and worker the men had actively used their meeting, the present moment, for engagement of themselves in active movement in directions that had meaning to them, and for increasing their sense of self-worth. The worker helped them use their current interest, their group, and their group meeting to develop a new sense of life and purposefulness.

HELPING THE GROUP TO RESPONSIBLE DECISION

Patterns of behavior and social attitudes do not change precipitately, but slowly, through the group work process, accelerated by the worker's activity in the context of each meeting of worker with group. Still seeking to identify the nature of the group work skill that may eventuate in a shift to the group members' new and more responsible use of themselves in their relationships to each other, the

agency, and society, we turn to our second piece of recorded material. Here the worker responded to the events
of the meeting by helping the members of the group
examine their methods of solving group problems, and
their responsibility to one of their members.

The "Kings" are a group of teen-age boys of a variety
of nationalities—Irish, Italian, Czech, etc.—living in a
middle-class, small urban community. In their immediate
neighborhood is a Jewish Community Center open to
Jews and non-Jews alike, but primarily serving Jewish
groups. The boys' introduction to the agency occurred
when they moved as a gang into and around the building,
not to join the agency but to explore it in their own
terms, disturbing the groups that were meeting there. In
two discussions with the Program Director the boys began
to make plans to meet regularly at the agency with staff
leadership, and were assigned a worker. The following
material is the worker's account of part of his third meeting with the Kings, at which fifteen boys were present.

The first part of the meeting was spent discussing the
report cards the boys had received at school that day, hearing reports of the secretary and treasurer, planning a
movie night at the agency, to be sponsored by the club,
clearing basketball dates, and considering their relation
with another group that was seeking a basketball game
with them. Then their attention was turned to one of
their members, Dan, whose behavior at the meeting precipitated an examination of their attitudes and of their
methods of making decisions.

. . . During the collection of dues, Dan was talking to the person next to him and Terry, the president, told him to "shut up." Dan gave him a somewhat defiant look but kept quiet. Terry told him he was custodian for the night (the one to clean up the room after the meeting). Dan said that he was not. Terry retorted that he was. There was only some mumbling on Dan's part.

Terry said that he had been discussing dues with some of the fellows and that there was a new rule that anybody who misses four meetings is out of the club. When nobody questioned this, I turned to George who has been working with the Constitution Committee, and asked him if this wasn't one of the things that the Committee planned to bring to the club for a vote. He said that it was and Terry suggested they wait then, until it comes up in the Constitution, but that he thought it was a good rule. . . .

As they discussed their need for a basketball coach, Dan said that he would be the coach. Terry told him to be quiet, that he was not called upon to speak and reminded him that he was already custodian for tonight. Dan replied, "If I'm custodian, then you are too." When Terry said that *he* makes the decision as to who is custodian, Dan again mumbled under his breath. . . .

Rudy slid backwards on his chair and an ash tray broke. After walking over to see if he had been hurt, I said it was a shame that the ash tray had been broken but I didn't think it was very expensive. Rudy proceeded to pick up the pieces and take them out of the room, with no comment from the other boys. I said I had noticed another ash tray which was broken and swept under a chair and I wondered what would happen about that one. Walter walked over and said, "I broke it, I'll clean it up." Dan, who was sitting near the broken tray, bent over and began to pick up the pieces and Terry told him to sit still and stay in the meeting. Dan continued with what he was doing and walked out of the room. As soon as he had left the room, Terry said, "How many guys think Dan ought to be voted out of the club?" There was general laughter and hubbub and a couple of hands went up. Terry said, "O.K., he's out." Dan walked in with a big smile, obviously having heard and said, "Am I out? O.K., I'm going," and left the room. Terry, in the midst of general laughter said, "I don't think a guy ought to stay in the meeting if he's going to mess it up all the time."

James wanted to know what was going to happen to Dan. Terry questioningly said, "We voted on it, didn't we?" Pat laughed, saying, "Very legal!" Terry said that it was Dan's own fault for messing around, and that anyway, he hates everybody in the club and everybody hates him, too. Pat said, "That's all right for you to say *here*," implying that there would be serious consequences if this comment were made to Dan.

Then there was a lull and Pat wanted to go on with the business. Terry agreed and started to proceed when I interrupted to ask, "What's going to happen with this situation?" Terry asked what I thought they should do but Pat interrupted to say, "It's not *his* club. *We* have to decide." I agreed that what Pat said was perfectly true but if they were throwing Dan out of the club because he walked out of the room, then this would have to apply to other members of the club, too. Rudy said, "I don't go for that; anybody is liable to walk out sometime." Terry said, "Dan thinks the club's a big joke; if he were serious, he'd have come back." George said, "Look, I don't like him any better than the rest of you guys but I don't think you can just put him out. Maybe we can make him want to quit."

Walter said, with his head down, "I don't like ex-cons." "But he paid for it," was James's reply, and Ted said that had nothing to do with this. There was a singular desire on the part of all the boys to move away from this topic. Dominic said, "Let's make him pay a fine." Terry agreed that this was a good idea; "Yeah, or else make him stay out of the club for two weeks." There was a moment of silence and I raised my hand to speak. I said that today all of them had received their report cards and I wondered what they would think if they were told to hand in a paper and when they handed it in late, the teacher flunked them for the entire course, and when they asked her about it, she would say, "That's a rule I have in my class." Pete said, "But they would tell you about the rule ahead of time." "Certainly," I said, "you would have a right to be sore if you were punished for something when you didn't know about the rule. Now isn't that what is happening here with Dan?"

Pat suddenly said, "Let's send somebody out to tell Dan to come back in," and Dude said that was the right thing to do. Ted was half way to the door when I stopped him. I asked him to sit down and I asked all of them what they were going to say to Dan. Dominic suggested they ask him how he was going to act from now on. Terry said to me, "See, the thing is, Jerry, you don't know him on the outside." Dominic added to this, "Yeah, we better send a couple of big guys to talk to him," and Terry continued with, "That's right, he's bigger than most of us and he's always giving us shots [hitting them] and even in the meeting when I tell him to do something, he mumbles to himself."

I said that they were right, I didn't know Dan on the

outside but that I did know some things that happened in the Center. What Dan had done tonight certainly did not make for a better meeting but then, again, several of the fellows had interrupted a number of times. I had also worked with Dan on the Constitution Committee and he had been very helpful there and was one of the people interested in starting the club.

Ted stood up and said, "Look, a lot of you guys hate him, and Terry, you have to admit that you and Pat are a bit prejudiced against him." Dude, who had been very quiet until now, rose ceremoniously to say, "I don't think it is fair to kick him out. He's no worse than some of the rest of us."

I nodded to Dude and said that I wondered if Ted might not be right, that because of some of the things that happened outside of the Center, some of the fellows were prejudiced against Dan. I then tried to clarify for them the role of the club in relation to individual contacts they might have outside of the club, ending with, "Certainly you can decide what you wish, but whatever you decide, then (1) it should apply to everyone else, and (2) you should think how hard or easy it might be for Dan to come back, depending on what you say to him."

Pete stood up, saying, "Let Ted and me go get him and we'll tell him just to come back—that the guys want him to come back." The boys agreed very quickly without taking a vote but I stopped the two from leaving and asked that Terry get a vote or more discussion as to whether they really wanted to ask Dan to return in this way. Terry put the question to a vote and there was unanimous agreement. When Pete and Ted left the room to look for Dan, there were reaffirming comments from several of the boys about this being the thing to do—". . . but if he acts up again!" At this point George said that we must make sure that all of us know the rules next time before we do anything.

As Dan came in, smiling, preceded by the other two, he was greeted by Terry's words, "You're custodian." "So are you," answered Dan, but Terry responded with, "I decided." Dan looked around the room and mumbled something. I asked Terry if it wasn't true that once a person was custodian, he wouldn't have a second turn until everyone had one. Terry said that was correct and Dan nodded. "But I'm going to make me last," Terry said and everyone laughed, including Dan.

Pat said that this was the lousiest meeting they had ever had and a couple of others echoed his feelings. I said I wasn't so sure about this. I thought every group would have arguments and disagreements but what was really important was how they handled their differences. I reminded them of their Constitution Committee; when their constitution was drawn up and agreed upon, there would be less opportunity for the kind of argument they had had today. . . . I reviewed the problem briefly that had arisen today and pointed out that the way they had finally handled it was a sign of a group that was interested in being a group and remaining a good one—a club that took time to discuss their differences and problems.

I asked about cleaning up, and Dan and three others immediately rushed to clean the ash trays and put the chairs in order. The rest of the boys left. I stayed to help clean up and used this opportunity to talk about the incident with Dan for a few minutes.

In this meeting are traces of the way these adolescent boys had been accustomed to solving their problems. A few of the strongest boys formulated new rules that were suddenly invoked in their meetings; if one member got out of line, they would summarily dismiss him or threaten him with physical violence. When the same impulsive behavior started to emerge now in this meeting, the worker consistently raised questions that engaged the boys in questioning their own procedures. An instance of this process occurred early in the meeting when the president announced that "some of the fellows" had made a new rule about absences; since none of the members objected, the worker referred to their new committee, implying that preparatory to a full group decision in an orderly manner, they already had a structure in which problems of this kind were being considered. He was suggesting that they use their new channels for making decisions. Regardless of their former practices which they had begun to discard, he was holding them to the new structures they were in the process of developing.

Similar evidence of their struggle between impulse and considered, more responsible behavior is seen in their reaction to the member's act of walking out of the meeting: quickly, the president, with the support of the others, produced a new rule. The worker helped them see that they could not create a rule impulsively to fit one member who displeased them, without applying the ruling to all. Agreeing to this, the boys quickly decided that the member could return, but again, this was an impulsive conclusion. The strongest part of the worker's help lay in the manner in which he held the boys to considering their decision, thereby helping them to change their method of affecting their group life. The limits implicit in their being fair to all members, in airing their feelings and opinions freely and fully, in examining alternatives—all of which the worker introduced and sustained—were instrumental in the group members' discovery of a new way to relate to each other. They were in a process of creating something new and enriching for themselves, namely, a way to come to a group decision in which all participated, a kind of action for which they could feel affirmatively responsible because they had truly taken a considered part in it. If the worker had silently accepted their quick, superficial shift in opinion, he would have been encouraging the perpetuation of their old, impulsive behavior. Here in the group meeting, in the present time with them, he was not only expecting that the boys could find new ways of relating to each other and could develop changing, more responsible methods of solving their group problems, but was active in helping them to achieve these goals.

In expressing their feelings against the recalcitrant member, the boys were full of their irritation and fear over what the boy was like outside of the club meetings, and over the fact that he had served a term in a correctional institution. The worker asked them to consider what the boy had been doing in their meetings as a club member, acknowledging that he had been disruptive today, as others of them were from time to time, but implying that they might weigh the value of a member by the kind of responsibility he takes for the club's affairs. He agreed with them that the decision in this matter was theirs, but helped them to weigh their decision by leading them to think of what they would say to the absent member when he returned to the room. Could they deal with him as a club member in today's meeting, rather than with someone they were prejudiced against because of some of his actions on the outside? The crisis past, it was one of the members who said, with a new sense of responsibility, "We must make sure that all of us know the rules next time!"

It is not enough to help a group take on more accountability for its actions and relationships, for it is equally important to help its members comprehend the value in what they have accomplished. Thus, before adjournment of the meeting, the worker met a member's criticism of the argumentative meeting by pointing out the way they had settled their disagreements on this day. This, he said, was a sign that they were "a group that took time to discuss their differences and problems." He was helping them possess what they had done in this meeting, and to claim their active part in its outcome.

The thesis of this chapter is simply this: the present is the time available to the worker for helping his group members, and to the members for discovering more creative use of themselves. In psychological terms, Otto Rank asserts that the present is the only anchor for the psychic life. "Thinking and feeling, consciousness and willing can always be only in the present." [2] The present is all that one can truly grasp. It is only the present, given moment of time that is available to a person for growth as he wills it.

This is not to deny the significant effect of former experience upon one's current life. The crux of the matter is how one *uses* his past in the present and how he uses the present to move forward toward the future that holds his goals and aspirations. What has gone before and what is to come meet in the present, at the pivotal point of human life.

It is that pivotal point, the present moment of time, that is available to the group worker for his help to group members in their use of relationships with each other and with himself. The continuous process between members and worker is necessarily set in the framework of current happenings. Each shift in activity, in behavior, in mood and attitude, demands that the worker meet it as it emerges. Group discussions include problematic feelings and attitudes whose roots are not in the group relations but which are current and pressing in the members' lives and shared to some extent by all of them. Questions of cultural difference, their own and others, attitudes about sex, about parents or children, social values, are illustrative of this kind of program content. With the immediacy and currency of these aspects of group interests, the worker's question is: What can I introduce, how can I respond to these group members so as to produce a dynamic moment of engagement as they consider issues that are real to them? Although the worker is conscious of his part in such a moment, he does not induce it falsely or artificially

—indeed, he has no need to—for engagement develops from the actual and real content of the group meeting and of the relationships that surround it.

Relative to the approach we have been describing, which emphasizes the present in time, is the practical question for the group worker as to what use he can make of information that comes to him regarding previous experiences of the group and its members, or whether he should seek such information. Certainly it contributes to understanding of the present to know something of how it came to be. There are, for example, groups that refer frequently to the previous year or years with comments like: "This club has never been any good!" or, "You should have seen us last year!" The worker, in such instances, responds with interest and concern to what they are telling him, discussing their feelings about it with them, but he moves on, surely and purposefully, to a focus on the present: "And what can you do in your group right now?"

In addition to what the worker may hear from the members, either singly or collectively, of their previous group experience, existing group or individual records may be available to him in the agency. From a perusal of records (and this is applicable, too, to information gleaned from the supervisor and other staff-members), the worker gains a sense of what the members were like in previous years, how they related to each other, the worker, and the agency; the program content of their meetings, their successes and their disappointments; something of their attitudes toward themselves and their group, their values.

It is likely that it would have a great deal of meaning to a group to discover that its new worker is interested enough in them to have learned something about their previous activities in the agency. This would be especially true if the members were proud of their achievements; but even though their program or their reputation around the agency was something they would like to hide, they would value the worker's indication of interest in them if they could feel it as that. The worker may be able to use whatever information he has about the group's previous connection with the agency to add to the members' sense of continuity which the agency and its function provide for them through the worker as its representative. With knowledge of the past the worker can help the members to claim and use what has gone before, which is part of his professional responsibility as a social worker. It must be assumed that the skillful worker will be free to find his unique relation to the group members, knowing that what each member is now being and experiencing in relation to him and the other group members is what he must work with, regardless of the problems or satisfactions that the members have had prior to this time.

For the inexperienced, untrained worker, such as the beginning student in training or the part-time session-leader, there are some dangers in acquiring knowledge about groups from the records of former workers. The temptation may be to repeat the past, both in content and expectation, or to try to pattern the present leadership after that of the former worker if it seems to have been effective. More serious is the tendency to see the group members as they *were* the previous year, through the eyes and reporting of another worker, with the expectation of a recurrence of former problems of relationships. Increasingly, common agency practice in regard to reading records is to ask the inexperienced worker, new to a group, to meet with the members several times, to gain his own impressions from his contact with them, and to form his own beginning relations with the members before turning to the records for whatever illumination they may give him. Beginning workers who have followed this procedure have sometimes been comforted to find evidence of the same problems and behavior patterns that they have already encountered in their current work; they have also been startled with the discovery that some of their members are relating to their present group and worker in very different ways—either more or less positively. As they have developed skill they have been increasingly able to make professional use of knowledge of the past so that it enhances, rather than hinders, the work with their groups.

Whitehead says tersely, ". . . the understanding which we want is an understanding of the insistent present." [3] The situational factors of the group, agency, and relationship with group members, testing, as they do, both the members' and the worker's use of the past in the present, comprise the "insistent present" for the group worker.

To lend one's self to the kind of helping which stems from the concept that the present in time is a vehicle for growth-producing relationships, requires of the worker a steady and tested conviction that every person has capacity for growth, and has inherent strength which sometimes only with help from another—an external, professional person—can become available for use. The core of the help lies in the worker's belief in the group members' strength, his readiness to sense it, and his freedom to engage the members in process with him and each other, in which they choose how they will use their strengths to the end that their inner forces are mobilized for forward movement.

In enabling the group members to carry their appropriate part of the process, the worker holds them to facing the reality of their present situation, sharpens the issues, presents his difference given him by the profession and agency which he represents, and conveys his genuine expectation that the members, through relationships set in motion by the situation of a given meeting, can make choices that will increase their personal strengths as they experience the exhilaration of deeper levels of responsibility for themselves.

Fleeting though the current, given moment of time is, it is invested with a deeply significant quality. "The present contains all that there is. It is holy ground; for it is the past, and it is the future." [4] The group worker who conceives of the present as containing "all there is," embodying both past and future, keeps his focus on the reality of his current relationships with his group members as he helps them develop new strengths and new levels of responsibility by facing the demands of the present.

CHAPTER NOTES

1. Daniel Grodofsky, "The Worker's Use of Structure and Function in Helping a Group of Older Adults Achieve More Responsible Group Relations," unpublished Master's Thesis, University of Pennsylvania School of Social Work, 1953.
2. Otto Rank, *Will Therapy and Truth and Reality* (New York: Knopf, 1945), p. 38.
3. Alfred North Whitehead, *The Aims of Education* (New York: Macmillan, 1929; Mentor Books, 1949), p. 14.
4. *Ibid.*, p. 14. This statement regarding the present has been paraphrased to read: ". . . the whole past is summed up in it, the future is implicit in it; and at its worst it contains the values and ideals that inspire men to condemn it." Herbert J. Muller, *The Uses of the Past* (New York: Oxford, 1952), p. x.

CHAPTER VI

Skill in Stimulating and Using
Group Relations

UP TO THIS POINT we have identified and discussed three
of the characteristics of social group work skill—the ability to use agency function, to communicate with members
on a feeling level, and to use the reality of the present
moment of time—all essential to the worker's competence
and effectiveness in helping group members achieve increasing self-responsibility and sense of self-worth. But
while these three constituents of skill have been examined
for their use in the group work process and their relation
to group work purpose, they are also intrinsic in the skill
of the social caseworker—a fact of which ample evidence
appears in the literature of functional casework. The
generic quality of the social worker's philosophic and psychological base for his responsible part in the social work
process is thus demonstrated, while allowing for the differences of the auspices through which he is offering his professional skill and the differences of the method, group
work or casework, that he is employing.

The one characteristic of social group work skill truly unique to it among the social work specializations is the stimulation and conscious use of group relations in process with the worker, toward the goal of social growth of the persons and groups served. We are cognizant of the recently accelerated development of work with groups of clients or patients in casework agencies, mental hospitals, and various kinds of treatment centers. In some instances such work is carried, not by a group worker, but by a caseworker or therapist. The purposes of, and therefore the approach to, these groups vary with the function of the agency as well as with the psychological concepts underlying the helping process. From a study of published accounts one would judge that the degree of conscious use of group relations also varies.[1] If the worker—caseworker, therapist, or group worker—is consciously focusing his effort on developing group relations and helping the members to use them, if he is able to give his attention to every member and also to the group as a whole, and if he is free to entrust part of the process to the engagement of the members with each other, he is employing the fourth and final aspect of social group work skill that has been selected for elaboration in this writing.[2]

As has been stated in the introductory pages of this volume, social group workers make no claim to have discovered the significance of the group in society or of the relations between members of a group. The nature of the social group and its effect on society as both carrier and recipient of values, and the effect on groups and society of various types of leadership, have long been focal points of study for other disciplines, such as sociology and applied anthropology. Of recent years, social psychology with its emphasis on group dynamics has contributed significantly to knowledge of the reciprocal effect of the group and individual participants, with special concern for the roles carried by various members.[3] The educational profession is giving renewed attention to the use of group relations as a means of carrying out its educational function.

GROUP RELATIONS AS THE FOCUS
FOR SOCIAL GROUP WORK PROCESS

Social group work as a specialization in the social work profession has focused its efforts on understanding and using the worker's activity in a process that enables each group member to find and take his part in the whole, in relationship with other members. With acknowledgment of the value of learnings of the other disciplines, on which group workers continually draw, we direct our attention now to the skill essential to the group worker if, consistent with the purpose of his profession, he is to direct the process of group relations to the end of helping each group member to develop a more responsible self, and the group as a whole to move toward socially responsible goals.

In any group of people meeting under any kind of auspices, relationships between the various members are operating. The bond between members may be most tenuous, may be negative or divisive, or may have the quality of positive connection that brings satisfaction to those who experience it. But responses between people in a group are an inevitable part of group associations. One has only to observe a group of children playing by themselves on a corner lot to corroborate this statement: they disagree with each other, they somehow choose what game they will play, and either by the forcefulness of one of their number or by some other method of decision, someone is accepted as "It" for their game. Adults, too, develop ways of relating to each other, of expecting certain kinds of responses from certain members, and devise their own ways of welding themselves into a group, of establishing themselves as parts of the whole group.

Reciprocal relations between group members, then, are not created by the social group worker, but are a factor to be understood, used, and developed to the enhancement of the participating members. Thus conceived, the group process, far from being obstructive to the group worker's fulfillment of his professional purpose, provides the central core for his work—a constructive, dynamic force which the worker can modify and strengthen if he possesses the skill to do so. For the social group worker deals with the social reality of the group before him—the group with all of the interpersonal relationships of its members. "Social work," wrote Kenneth Pray, "is never primarily concerned with the separate, inner, personal life or development of the individual as such, but always with his relation to the outer social realities in which he is involved. Even in social casework—and still more obviously in social group work or community work—the criterion of the effectiveness of its service is not what kind of person this individual in himself has come to be, but how he is relating himself to the situation in which he finds himself, to the values and responsibilities these relationships hold for him." [4]

Multiplying the relation of one individual to the rest of the group by the number of persons present, each with different reactions, there results a complexity of relationships for the group worker's concern. In addition to helping each individual to find his part in the whole, the worker is also responsible for developing the group as a whole. Dewey speaks of "unity in variety. . . . The formula has meaning only when its terms are understood to concern a relation of energies. There is no fullness, no many parts, without distinctive differentiations. . . . The 'one' of the formula is the realization through interacting parts of their respective energies. The 'many' is the manifestation of the defined individualizations due to opposed forces that finally sustain a balance." [5]

The worker carries the responsibility for helping group members seek and sustain a balance in their group relations that provide both unity and diversity for them. For it is the worker whose presence and activity add focus and control to the process of group relationships. To carry the control of a process that allows and enables group members to have their full and appropriate part in the process, so that the outcome is their own, requires skill, and we will proceed to identify the components of this particular aspect of social group work skill.

In the area of awareness, the worker must be conscious of every member of the group, and not become absorbed with the members who are the most vocal or demanding. His relation to each member is important, but if he is to accelerate the group relations and help members to use them, he will need to modify the many diverse, individual strands of his relationship with the members so that they will be in process with each other and so that he will have a connection with the group as a whole. Grace Coyle has referred to this relation to a group with an apt simile: the worker cannot be like a Maypole to which each ribbon is firmly and separately attached.[6]

THE USE OF PROGRAM TO STRENGTHEN GROUP RELATIONS

The worker's focus on relating members to each other may be conveyed by external action as well as by verbalization. A pertinent example of unspoken help follows in the account of a few minutes of a meeting of nine-and-ten-year-old boys. A boy called Johnson was silent and fearful, unable up to the time of this meeting to risk himself in relationship with the other boys of the group, except in most tentative ways. For several weeks, the worker had helped the boy to trust him, with the aim of helping him to trust himself sufficiently to find an active part in the group. Now the worker records:

> The club seemed excited and ready for action and when Joe put on a square-dance record, Johnson caught hold of my two hands and started swinging me around. Dick and Arnold also began to swing around with each other and then John and Joel. Dave was standing in the middle of the three swinging pairs and I swung Johnson into Dave

and withdrew from the circle. They continued circling around for several minutes. . . . As all the boys said good-by to me at the end of the meeting, Johnson left the room with the others. This was the first time that he had not waited for me. . . .

In this sensitive, wordless fashion, the worker, through the group's program, helped a member become related to the group he had chosen and conveyed his expectation that the boy would carry his part with the others.

Group members relate to each other around a common purpose or interest, finding in a co-operative venture the channel for initiating and cementing relations with each other. This is one of the several purposes for the use of recreational activities in group work practice. Here the worker who is aware of this aim will help groups select those program activities that will facilitate stronger relations between members. As one group work educator points out, the wall newspaper or the group mural is more appropriately group work activity than is the painting or the leather object made separately by each member for his private use.[7]

Those who have shared in group activities, been part of a group decision, or contributed to the growth of a communal idea know the satisfaction and exhilaration of such an experience. There is no mechanical way of describing group process as it evolves around activities or issues or ideas, for it develops as people relate to each other and is creative only as its participants find expression for their real selves and are free to take in, and respond to, the real feeling and ideas of others.

Agnes deMille writes vividly of the dependence of the choreographer on the creative skill and expression of the dancers. "The dancers themselves frequently help. For the very reason they are human and have wills and imaginations and styles of their own, their manner of moving will suggest an infinite number of ideas to the choreographer. They can evoke where clay and canvas cannot. . . . A sensitive performer needs only a hint, a breath, and he is off, the rhythms generated in his body helping to push the design ahead. . . . Such times are memorable. . . . In this art, the interpreters are present at the actual moment of creation and if they share the labor they also know some of the glory." [8]

And so can it be, through various media, in social group work where the participants, if enabled by the worker to share the labor, can also know some of the glory. In the realm of ideas and decisions, when all members are engaged in the process of developing them, each contributes, takes in something from other members, shifts a little, giving up something of what he has previously held, thereby gaining more for himself—until in a continuous process a group idea emerges, sometimes as clear as crystal in form, sometimes amorphous. But each person who has participated in the development of it knows that it has become a group idea, built of individual expressions and responses, of differences and agreements, and that it has required some change in all who had part in it. "The creative process is the process of change, of development, of evolution, in the organization of subjective life." [9]

The social group worker's part in process is not only to be sensitively attuned to the process that the members are engaged in, but to help them develop it by responding to the real feelings that underlie the members' expressions, by introducing the difference of his ideas and of his own and the agency's values, by helping them to hold to a focused content in discussion. Only so can the worker help the group members through their group relations to move toward the change, development, and evolution of which Ghiselin speaks as the characteristic of creative process.

Containment—an Essential Quality in the Worker

But in addition to the active, verbal part that is the worker's function to carry as he stimulates and directs the group relations, is a conscious deliberateness in allowing the members to interact without his manifest participation. Containment is a word that describes an important and difficult quality that the worker must possess if he is to use group relations to their maximum effectiveness. This quality is not to be equated with passivity that simply allows the group members to drift aimlessly. It is, rather, the active and conscious use of restraint that stems from the philosophic belief that not only do people have strengths within themselves, but that only as the human will is engaged can there be forward movement. The worker must believe that the group members have something substantial to give to each other and must be willing to let them relate to each other as they will, which is one aspect of enabling them to do so. Skill is possessed when the worker is able with sureness to select when he will be active and when, in silence, he will let the group carry the process.

For the purpose of examining how this aspect of skill—containment—may be translated into practice, a record is presented in the following pages. A second thread of inquiry to be followed in studying this recorded material is the effect of group relations on the single member that leads him to new freedom to come to responsible decisions and action. In relation to both of these points, we will seek to identify evidences of the worker's skill.

The material comes from the service and agency described in an earlier chapter, the Pre-Parole Service of the Social Service Department of a large State Mental Hospital.[10] Of a series of eight meetings with a group of patients who were exploring their readiness to make plans for leaving the hospital, this was the sixth meeting. The next major step for each patient who had already chosen to leave through Foster Care was to appear before the Social Planning Staff, in which doctors and social workers participate. The worker records:

Most of the men arrived at approximately the same time. When the attendant brought Mr. Roberts and Mr. Downs, she said that Mr. Downs had been asking for several days now when he would be seeing "that man from Social Security." Mr. Downs, for the first time, looked really pleased at seeing me and the group. The others laughed good-naturedly at his error, explaining that I was the Social Service man. To this, Mr. Downs replied that he didn't

care what they called me so long as they knew that I was
the person he wanted to see—"the man who helped."

There was a loaded silence in the group now with a certain amount of looking around with wonder and surprise
at the smaller size of the group. Someone meekly commented on how small the group was now and I picked it
up, saying that I guessed they were feeling the change, for
the group was truly different. They might well have some
feeling about it, thinking perhaps that I had taken some
of their friends out of the group and they might be angry
with me. Mr. Kaye commented that the group was surely
different but he didn't have any feeling about it one way
or another. The others agreed with him and I wondered
then if they might not mind being left behind, not having
proceeded so rapidly as some of the rest. Mr. Adams said
that he expected to be left behind because he had started
later than the others, but Mr. Kaye reminded him that they
had all begun at the same time.

Now Mr. Hale sparked the group into telling some of
their discomfort at the change they found in the group.
They were particularly hurt by feeling left behind and not
moving as quickly as those who were no longer there. When
everyone (except Mr. Small, who was silent) had expressed
some of their concern, I told them I thought it was good
they could share their feelings with me, even ones that were
not the most pleasant; but then, wasn't life, weren't people,
made up of both the pleasant and unpleasant? Could they
find something to move ahead on?

Mr. Kaye said he thought each one of them was different
and that they moved at different rates of speed, so some had
to be behind the others. Mr. Vale said they had each had a
part with me in deciding the dates to appear before the

Planning Staff and he felt that a later date for him was his own choice. Now Mr. Adams, who has been procrastinating on a date for Staff, said, "Mr. Case, aren't you forgetting something?" When I looked puzzled, he said that now he was the only one who didn't have a date and he proceeded to make one for himself.

Mr. Hale said he knew that not everyone could come before Staff at the same time, for there would be people from the women's group, too. And he went on to tell of how he has used the additional time to prepare further for appearing before the Staff. From all this, they came out with general agreement that some could move more rapidly than others, as was true for life on the outside, and they would live with it here as they would have to do in the community, though they might not like it.

I wondered if they might find it difficult to leave the group or the hospital. Mr. Downs said, "Shucks, no!"—he wanted to get out of this place and the sooner the better. The others, spurred by their desire to leave and their fear of facing the problem of leaving, quickly agreed with him. I asked if maybe there wasn't some problem for us whenever we left anything we were used to. Mr. Hale said he never has any trouble with good-bys. Mr. Kaye said, "You know, if you ever had to leave your home and family, you know how hard it was to do, even though you had to do it to grow up!" With deep feeling, Mr. Vale then agreed and said that a person kind of got used to the group meetings and the people and the social worker. Mr. Adams told how they got into the routine of the hospital, the food, the nurses and attendants. Now the whole group let themselves feel some of the pain of ending with the group, the hospital, and myself. Each man in his own way showed real insight and depth of feeling.

I then said I wondered what could help them with these endings they were facing. Mr. Kaye said that if you could just remember that you were leaving to get a new and different way of life, you could stand it. Mr. Roberts, who had been sitting stooped, red-eyed, and mostly silent, said that he was looking forward to a Foster Home, though this would be second-best for him. He hoped it would be better than the hospital.

Now a barrage of questions came about their appearance before Staff. What should they wear, how should they talk, etc.? Mr. Hale nicely put the meaning of these questions when he said that he was very confident—he has faced many strangers in his life and he will be O.K. with the doctors and social workers at Planning Staff. I asked how the rest felt, for I wondered if some of their questions weren't the results of some anxiety over the prospect of coming before Staff. Mr. Adams said that no matter how many times he went to Staff, he was always scared until he had talked for a while. Mr. Vale pointed out that he was a veteran at it but he still gets nervous. They all laughed with nervousness and relief.

I asked if there was anything more they could do that would be of help to them, not to do away with the anxiety, for it was good that they could own it, but that would help some so that they wouldn't be immobilized. Mr. Adams said that he would tell the truth and know it was the truth— what more could be asked? Mr. Kaye said that he would tell the Staff what he had done to get ready for it. And now the others, each in his own way, told what he had been doing in preparation for Staff and said that thinking about it helped them live with the normal anxiety they had. Mr. West, seeing everyone move ahead so quickly, mobilized himself with a plan to see the doctor and get a date for Staff, too. . . .

The patients at this meeting faced three important features of their social reality: the realization that some patients, former members of their group, had already moved ahead of them to leave the hospital; their own imminent separation from the group and the hospital; the threatening prospect of appearing before the Social Planning Staff. Looking for the pattern of the process in this meeting, one finds that in each of the three instances the worker initiated and focused the discussion by identifying and expressing for the group members the feelings he anticipated they might be having, speaking in a tentative and questioning way that stimulated the men to think about it and respond in their own terms, and that reminded them of the reality of their situation. The response of one member was the next step in the process, sometimes negative and disagreeing, but opening the way for others to express their opinions. The process continued as more and more members, encouraged by the participation of the others, were free to add their agreement or difference of feeling and in so doing to modify the group opinion at the same time that their own attitudes were undergoing change through finding new resolution in themselves to take another responsible step. It was during this part of the process that the worker contained himself to let the members work out their problems for themselves with each other's help and encouragement. It is apparent that he could let them carry the movement for several minutes at a time. But each time, the worker brought them back to a common focus by presenting a forward-moving question that asked them what they could do next, helping them to partialize the feeling that was developing and to consider specific steps or to affirm the steps they had already taken.

The affirmation of the different and responsible self that can result from this kind of process is clearly evident in this meeting. The men came to accept the reality that each of them was different from the others in tempo and in ability to make plans. They could say that they did not like some things, but could acknowledge that they themselves had a responsible part in their movement—slow or rapid—out of the hospital. They faced the fact that if they wanted to find "a new way of life," they would have to give up something, the comfortable familiarity of the hospital. All of this came clearer to them, along with the courage to express it and the resolution to move ahead in their preparation for leaving, through a process of relating to each other. They were stimulated to develop and use those relationships by the worker's skill that focused their attention on the realities of their social situation in this Pre-Parole group. His focus and his connection with the members of the group gave him freedom to select the appropriate times to direct the process actively or to let them carry the major part of it.

These men became a group through their common interest in preparing themselves to move out of the hospital. Such a group was deliberately formed by the agency as

time-limited, with awareness of the dynamic for movement in a defined span of time. The worker's purpose was
to help patients test and increase their ability to take responsibility for themselves, preparatory to parole from the
hospital; this purpose he endeavored to achieve through
the group work process. The purpose here did not encompass the development of the group as a whole for socially desirable ends in which the group as an entity
would have impact on society. In fact, the opposite was
true: the group service was offered with the single intent
that the individual members might use it to develop
enough purpose and strength in themselves to be able to
leave the group and the hospital. In this respect, the work
with this group was atypical of group work as it exists in
traditional group work agencies. But the aim of developing the group and a clear consciousness of it for the dura-
tion of its limited existence as a group was definitely held
by the worker and agency. If personal, individual strength
and self-value are to be gained from participation in the
group, there must be an awareness of common focus
among the members and identification of each one present with the others as a member of the given, specific
group. Hence, the worker's purpose includes helping the
group members to establish themselves as a group unit,
although temporary in nature.

GROUP RELATIONS IN CRISIS

In most of the recorded material presented in the preced-
ing chapters, there is evidence both of the worker's efforts
to enable the members to modify and use their relation-

ships to each other and of the movement toward achieving purpose that resulted from those efforts, although at the point that the records appear in this study, our discussion was focused on aspects of group work skill other than the use of group relations. One final record of a group meeting appears in the following pages, selected as particularly illustrative of the significance of group relations, even when fraught with conflict, as they may contribute to the development of the group as a whole and to the accompanying social responsibility and self-value of its members. Again we will seek to identify the worker's skill that enabled the group to move toward its own and the agency's purposes.

The record that follows is of a special meeting of a teen-age (fourteen–eighteen) girls' chapter of a national youth organization. The meeting was planned and called by a few of the active older members for the purpose of ousting the younger girls who had recently joined the group, or of considering the establishment of a separate chapter for them. When one of the older girls, Sharon, telephoned the worker to invite her to attend the meeting of the older faction, the worker said that this was a problem that affected the whole club and that unless all members were notified of the meeting and its purpose, she could not attend. Sharon agreed to tell the rest, including the president, Mildred, whose recent illness led Sharon to want to protect her. A little later Mildred, too, called the worker, sounding hurt at what she felt as intended exclusion of herself. She said she was going "to have a showdown" at the meeting and would bring all of the younger, new members with her. The worker assured her that she also would be present, since all or most of the members were coming.

In the recorded account of the meeting as it took place, we are concerned with the way in which the worker helped the eighteen girls present to assess, modify, and use their relations to each other as they worked through the conflict that threatened their existence as a chapter.

When I arrived at Florence's house at seven o'clock I found Rachel, Esther, and Florence talking about school. They were surprised to see me, since they had understood that I wasn't coming. I asked them if my coming upset them and they said no, that they wanted me to be present because I could help them decide what needed to be done. I said I would surely try to help the girls come to a decision that they could all agree upon and that I thought it was a good thing that the whole matter was to be discussed. The three girls wanted the chapter to continue but felt there should be a lower age limit for all new members after this meeting.

Other girls started to arrive in small groups and I greeted them all and in one way or another tried to help them to see that this was a positive step they were taking, and I tried also to do away with the tone of conspiracy that seemed to permeate each group of girls at they came in. When Mildred, the president, arrived with three of the younger and new members, pandemonium broke loose. Clumps of girls rushed over to me to ask if they should suspend the whole thing. I asked them what that would accomplish except to prolong the mixed-up feelings. They all expressed in various ways their feeling that the younger girls would be hurt. I asked if they didn't think that since the new girls had a stake in the problem, it would be a better idea to hear what they thought, too, and that they all might feel better for having shared in whatever decision they came to. They agreed and Effie asked who would be the spokesman for the older members. Sharon said that she would be, since she had raised the question in the first place.

The girls asked if I would chair the meeting and I agreed, thinking this would be good, since Mildred seemed so upset that I thought she would have difficulty being chairman and might easily jeopardize her relationship with the total group if she expressed herself in the way she seemed ready to do. I called the meeting to order and said that I was glad that so many of the girls were present because I knew that they all wanted to come to a decision that represented their combined thinking. I knew they had planned this meeting a little differently and were upset by the changes that had occurred in the past few days. This was not going to be easy and it would be hard on everyone, especially because they did not want to hurt anyone's feelings and were really concerned about the chapter and each other. There seemed to be a murmur of acceptance and I asked Sharon if she wanted to begin by telling in detail what this meeting was all about.

Sharon got up and moved to the edge of the circle to address the group. She started by saying she was sorry that the new members might have their feelings hurt but she felt that it was in the interest of the chapter to decide whether the newer members should start a new chapter or to limit the age of additional members to the ages of sixteen to eighteen and not concern themselves with a new chapter. She said that since they were essentially interested in social activities, the younger girls would be at a disadvantage, since they could not go with the older boys and the dates they had just did not seem to mix. She cited the recent party at Dora's house as an example. When she asked if she were stating the situation correctly, Effie agreed with her. Mildred objected violently and went into an impassioned denunciation of Effie and Sharon for making an issue out of the situation. She pointed out that the planned program calendar did not include any chapter socials and that their attitude was unreal. She personally favored having younger active members because they would perpetuate the group when the older members moved out to the Young Women's division. She reminded Effie, Rosalie, and Eve that they were only fourteen when they joined.

Eve granted Mildred's point and said that she agreed with her but that at that time the program was very different and fourteen-year-olds had no difficulty in fitting in. Hertha said that it was silly to judge people on the basis of age when really it was experience that mattered. She felt that some fourteen-year-olds could fit into this group very well socially. Rosalie said that she did not think she wanted to associate with young girls, since she was primarily interested in having successful socials while she was in the chapter.

There was cross-discussion and a great deal of mixed feeling was expressed but when I reminded the girls that each had a right to contribute her opinion, things would quiet down for a while. Several times I had to interrupt some really caustic exchanges between Effie and Mildred. The consensus of opinion seemed to be that from now on the age limit should be from fifteen to eighteen years and that if the membership were filled in, in this way, the chapter could continue permanently. Hertha and Esther felt that the younger girls who had already been voted in should be kept in the chapter. I picked up on this point and helped the girls to see that they had a responsibility to the people who had been accepted into the club and that if they wanted to set a new age limit, it might be better to do it from now on and not to renege on something they had already done.

At the beginning of the meeting there had been strong feeling that Mildred should not have brought the new, young members to this meeting. Esther was close to tears when she said that they ought not be hurt. Some of the others agreed and I said I knew this was painful, not only for the new members but for the other girls too. I asked if the three girls might not want to say how they felt about being present. Sharon objected and said that it was not fair to ask them. Rosalie said they could still leave if they wanted to, and Effie said they couldn't leave without admitting defeat. Sandra said she wanted the new girls to know she would not have come if she had known they were to be present. But Marcia said she would not have come if they were *not* there. I said it seemed to be time to ask what the three newer girls thought. Rebecca spoke up and said she was glad she had come, even though she hoped that never again in her whole life would she have to go through this kind of experience. She would much rather be present when she was being discussed than be told of a decision later. Carol and Elfrieda agreed with her and said they were glad they were in on the decision. I said to the whole group that as their advisor I was glad the whole matter had been discussed openly.

Florence suggested that each girl, one at a time, give her opinion. I asked if the comments and opinions could cover what seemed to me the three points under discussion and I listed them, asking the girls to correct me if they felt that I was missing or misstating anything. I listed (1) age limit; (2) what about the new members; (3) voting policy. They agreed that these were the main issues.

Sherry said she felt this whole discussion would have been unnecessary if, way back at the beginning of the year, the chapter had worked out clearer membership policies. Effie said that she had tried to bring this to a meeting but Mildred, the president, had not included it in the agenda. Sherry said, "Who's Mildred? Only the president—and if you want to raise something at the meeting, you can and if the rest want to talk about it, they do and if they don't, they don't." She turned to Mildred and said that she didn't mean this as an attack on her but she was talking about the duties of a president as such. I said that Sherry had an excellent point but that as advisor, I, too, had some responsibility in this. I had no idea that the age limits were bothering them and if I had known, I might have been able to help before the problem reached the point it had this evening. One of my reasons for being their advisor was to help the members make this group what they wanted it to be, after looking at all that was involved in the decisions they jointly made. They nodded their agreement and Eve said that I couldn't know what no one told me and that they could always bring up something important in a meeting. I said that a club was the responsibility of everyone who had anything to do with it—the members, the officers, and the advisor, and I hoped this discussion had given a much clearer idea of the part all three play in making the chapter a success.

After the one-by-one expression of opinion, the girls re-affirmed their earlier agreement that all present members should be retained but that for the future, the lower age limit should be fifteen. By this time there was a much better feeling in the room and people who had started out the evening disagreeing were now talking to each other in much more friendly tones. Sharon and Effie came to me later and said they were glad it was settled, although they still felt that sixteen would be a better age limit. I said I knew it was difficult for them to compromise on this point, since they had real feeling that the narrower age limit would be better for the chapter. But I wondered if they could concede to the general opinion that had been ex-pressed tonight. They said they certainly could because they believed in majority rule. I thought it was not so much a matter of majority rule as a common opinion that had been reached after discussing it thoroughly and looking at all sides of the question. Sharon agreed and said she prob-ably wouldn't be a close friend of any of the younger girls but that she would work with them all right. Effie said, "The same goes for me." I said that this was a really ma-ture way for them to feel and I knew they would be able to carry through on it. No one can be expected to be friends with everyone all the time, but they could all co-operate in relation to the chapter and perhaps, in time, they could know and even like the younger girls and not feel as doubtful of them as they did this evening.

Mildred had expressed hostility and anger through most of the evening, feeling that the whole question had been a maneuver against her. I recognized what her feelings were but was unable to make much headway in helping her lose some of her anger. I knew that I would see her at the office at the Council Meeting on the following evening and asked her if she could arrive early so that we could talk over further plans for the chapter. She agreed to my proposal.

The girls left in twos and threes and all stopped to say a few words to me, to finish expressing some of their feelings. Mainly, there seemed to be a strong sense of relief, comfort that now the discussion was over, and satisfaction that they had done the right thing.

Most of these girls came to the meeting with an already well-developed sense of the meaning of this chapter as a group with a long tradition of eight years of organization, which they, as the current, active members, hoped to perpetuate responsibly. As individuals they wanted to be assured that the chapter would provide the group activities they were seeking, and they feared that because of the diversity of ages and conflicting program interests, the group could not continue. A few of the girls, new to the group and uncertain of their status in it, were, with the support of the president, struggling to maintain a membership position, and undoubtedly were hoping to achieve firmer acceptance of themselves as wanted and necessary for the continuation of the group. The relations between these two subgroups were strained and ready to break.

What was the skill of the worker that helped the girls leave the meeting with a sense of "relief, comfort, and satisfaction"? At the outset her refusal to attend a meeting to which only some of the members were invited indicated to them that she valued the group as a unit and was ready to help them talk through the differences of the struggling factions. She conveyed her expectation that they were capable of coming to a solution by discussing the problem fully together.

Knowing that the girls were, on one hand, confused, guilty, and angry, and on the other, truly concerned with what happened to each member and anxious to have a stable, co-operative group, the worker met both sides of their feeling. Her part was to clarify the issues, to keep them focused on specific questions, to insist that everyone be heard, to encourage them to speak freely, and to respond to their earnestly stated opinions and feelings. Here, too, was containment, for the worker did not force the issue or express her own judgment. By both her attitude and vocal response to the girls she helped them to engage actively in solving their problem, often picking up and forwarding their own ideas, especially in regard to their sense of responsibility to each member and their continuous concern over what would be best for the club. So certain was the worker's direction toward enabling the girls to work out their problems in relation to each other that she was free to assume the chair for the meeting, without fear of dominating it, that she might be better able to hold the heated discussion to a focus and to help all members to participate freely.

Through the experience of discovering that they had the freedom and the primary responsibility to face and deal with the group crisis, the girls began to see the stake that every other member had in the health of the club, to feel themselves as part of a whole, and to move toward more responsible, group-centered concern. In this process, where every opinion was valued by the worker and, to an increasing extent, by the members, the self-value of each participant was enhanced. The group relations shifted from a blaming, guilty, or hurt quality to an open, sharing quality as they examined every expression of opinion, considered opposing arguments and other people's feelings, and finally came together on a solution to the problem that was so real to them.

The cornerstone of a group worker's skill in helping members use group relations is trust, not only that interaction between people is possible, but that the process of interrelationships in a group can be creative, providing opportunities for the participants to gain increased sense of their own personal worth and direction for themselves as responsible, contributing parts of a whole. Grace Coyle expresses the philosophic basis for the results of such group relations: "Because of man's essentially social nature his fullest growth comes only as he uses his expanding powers in conjunction with and for the benefit of others." [11]

Skill in developing and using group relations to achieve the purpose of social group work stems from the worker's readiness to sense and accept the process that goes on between members of a group, his conviction of the potentialities for growth in participation in group relationships, and his freedom to confine his own activity at appropriate times to responses to the members and to contributing a focus and professional difference around which the members can relate to each other with benefit to themselves and their group. The social group worker indeed controls the process of group relations but not the members, by enabling them to take their active and appropriate part in it.

CHAPTER NOTES

1. For example, Harris B. Peck and Virginia Bellsmith, *Treatment of the Adolescent* (New York: Family Welfare Association of America, 1954); Elsa Leichter, "Family Casework Through the Group Method," *Journal of Jewish Communal Service*, XXXII, Summer, 1956, pp. 376–387.

2. In the writer's opinion, the combined elements of this aspect of social group work skill are achieved only with extreme difficulty by one who has not undergone professional training for social group work.

3. For example, Dorwin Cartwright and Alvin Zander, editors, *Group Dynamics, Research and Theory* (Evanston, Ill.: Roe, Peterson, 1953).

4. Kenneth L. M. Pray, "Social Work in a Revolutionary Age," in *Social Work in a Revolutionary Age, and Other Papers* (Philadelphia: University of Pennsylvania Press, 1949), p. 237.

5. John Dewey, *Art as Experience* (New York: Putnam, 1934), p. 161.

6. Grace L. Coyle, "The Role of the Faculty Member in the Creation of an Integrated Program," unpublished paper presented at the 33rd annual meeting of the American Association of Schools of Social Work, New York, January 30, 1952.

7. Ruth R. Middleman, "Arts and Crafts as a Group Centered Program," *The Group*, December, 1954, pp. 16–26.

8. Agnes deMille, *Dance to the Piper* (Boston: Little, Brown; Atlantic Monthly Press book, 1952), pp. 313-315.

9. Brewster Ghiselin, editor, *The Creative Process, A Symposium* (Berkeley and Los Angeles: University of California Press, 1952), p. 2.

10. Cf. Chapter IV, page 114, Note 5.

11. Grace L. Coyle, *Group Experience and Democratic Values* (New York: Woman's Press, 1947), p. 32. Reprinted by permission of Whiteside, Inc., New York.

Conclusion

Our introduction states as an assumption that between social group work purpose and skill there is a reciprocal relation; defined purpose gives direction to the skill of the worker who is to approach the aims of group work; and skill, so directed, contributes to the fulfillment of the purpose. After considering the roots of group work skill, its purpose, and its philosophic base, we have given particular attention to the examination of selected specific aspects of skill—the use of agency function, communication, the present moment of time, and group relations— and to an analysis of the methods by which the worker uses these areas of skill to further movement toward the two major purposes of group work, namely, the individual growth of group members and the development of the group as a whole for social usefulness.

From the foregoing analysis of selected illustrations of group work practice as recorded by both professional and student workers, one can conclude that as the worker focuses on the purposes of group work, he selects a particular kind of pattern for his work with groups. It is a pattern which provides and forwards a process that engages the group members in exercise of choice and helps them relate to others. It provides opportunity for increased sense of self-value and for increasingly responsible attitudes and actions in relation to, and in conjunction with, other people. Were the purposes of a different character, other patterns would be selected. Group work goals require the development of structures that will facilitate a process through which group members can move toward these goals.

The universal factor in all the aspects of skill which we have been considering is the nature and degree of process that determines the effectiveness of the skill in fulfilling group work purpose. Process connotes interaction. In physical terms, it is the movement between two or more substances in which organic change occurs in reaction to an external force. In human society, the word denotes dynamic movement or interaction between one or more persons or groups. In social group work, process means that group members and worker are actively involved in reaction to each other in movement toward a defined goal. The worker's responsibility is to ensure process, introducing the difference of his professional understanding, his values, and the stability of the agency, to which the members can respond, and continuously enabling the members to participate in the movement of the group. At times, the worker initiates. At others, he accelerates. At still others, he contains himself, trusting the group members to strengthen themselves as they move in whatever direction they will. But regardless of his specific activity, the worker will hold a conscious and steady sense of the need for engagement of the members in active consideration of, and participation in, all matters that affect their group life. A condensed definition of group work skill, therefore, is the possession of a sense of process and capacity to direct process, respond to it, contain one's self to the end of achieving a balance of interacting forces within it. Group work skill is the ability to work in process with a group of people toward a clearly focused goal.

Group work skill, once possessed by a worker, is available for his use with a group in any setting where the purposes are consistent with basic social work values. Previous reference has been made to group work that is being done in institutions, such as hospitals and treatment centers. During the past ten years there has been steady and fairly rapid growth in the use of group work as a method of achieving agency purpose in institutions whose primary service is other than service to groups.[1] But group work skill is not limited to use in social agencies, for churches, schools, and community organizations profit from leadership which holds and uses the basic concepts that we have identified as essential to social group work skill. The values and concepts that give direction to group work practice are universal in their applicability, and the use of them in various settings depends on the worker's ability to identify with whatever may be the aims and functions of the institution or organization.

As the concept of the reciprocal nature of social group work purpose and skill has unfolded, criteria related to the fulfillment of purpose have emerged for the analysis of any piece of group work practice in terms of evaluating the skill of the worker. Criteria for skill are suggested by the following questions in regard to the worker's use of:

I. *Limitations imposed by the setting*

Does he view the agency function as providing scope and depth, rather than confinement and rigidity, for his help to people? Does the worker represent his agency's function in his work with groups? Is he able to use the function, hold to it, and convey its meaning to his group members?

II. *Communication*

Is the worker sensitive to the feelings of the people with whom he works? Does he consider feeling a reality to be acknowledged and dealt with? Does he convey his own feelings in a spontaneous but responsible way?

III. *The present in time*

Does the worker enable the members of his group to face the demands, the choices, the decisions of the present reality? Can he trust himself to stay with the immediate, to respond to it?

IV. *Group relations*

Can the worker help his members establish and modify relations between each other? Has he accepted and gained strength from the insistent and dynamic fact that he cannot carry the whole of the process but is dependent upon what the members can, and choose to, give and take in response to each other? Does his control of the process center on enabling the group to take its appropriate part in it and to use group relations for ongoing movement?

To meet any one of these criteria of skill, isolated from the others, cannot be considered as possession of social

group work skill. One aspect of skill can be used helpfully only if it is interwoven with the use of all the others.
The recorded material of the foregoing pages, while selected and discussed to demonstrate one particular area
of skill, reveals in each instance the need for the simultaneous use and integration of all components. Social group
work skill is possessed by a worker who has the demonstrated capacity to focus concurrently on all of its aspects.

We return, in conclusion, to the relation between social group work purpose and skill. Moving from the assumption that the two are reciprocal, through the analysis
of selected illustrations of group work practice and
through consideration of some of the values and theories
underlying this practice, we have evidenced that purpose
does provide direction for the practice, and that skill, so
directed and used, contributes to the fulfillment of the
purpose. Skill—"the capacity to set in motion and control
a process of change in the material . . . with consideration
for and utilization of the quality and capacity of the material" [2]—includes the comprehension and acceptance of
purpose, and active movement toward it.

The skillful social group worker uses his capacities in
the service of others in a process of helping people to gain
in self-value and social responsibility through their participation in groups.

CHAPTER NOTES

1. A study conducted by W. L. Kindelsperger, "Employment characteristics of the recent group work graduates, 1950–51–52," National Social Welfare Assembly, New York, 1953, reveals that of
   the total number of graduates (430) 76.9% were currently em-

ployed in traditional group work agencies; 14.0% in nontraditional settings; and the remainder not in group work or not employed. In the nontraditional settings, 26.5% were employed in medical and psychiatric hospitals; 17.2% in children's institutions; and the rest scattered in a variety of agencies.

See also Harleigh B. Trecker, editor, *Group Work in the Psychiatric Setting*, Proceedings of an Institute conducted by the American Association of Group Workers, 1955 (New York: Whiteside, and Morrow, 1956).

2. Virginia P. Robinson, "The Meaning of Skill," *Training for Skill in Social Casework* (Philadelphia: University of Pennsylvania Press, 1942), pp. 11–12.

Bibliography

SOCIAL GROUP WORK

Books and Pamphlets (Selected)

American Association of Group Workers. *Toward Professional Standards* (Selected papers for the years 1945 to 1946). New York: American Association of Group Workers; distributed by Association Press, 1947.

Coyle, Grace L. *Group Work with American Youth.* New York: Harper & Brothers, 1948.

———. *Group Experience and Democratic Values.* New York: The Woman's Press, and Whiteside, Inc., 1947.

Kaiser, Clara A., ed. *Objectives of Group Work.* New York: Association Press, 1936.

Klein, Alan F. *Society, Democracy and the Group.* New York: Woman's Press, 1953.

Konopka, Gisela. *Group Work in the Institution.* New York: Whiteside, Inc., and William Morrow & Company, 1954.

———. *Therapeutic Group Work with Children.* Minneapolis: University of Minnesota Press, 1949.

Murray, Clyde E., Bowens, Marx G., and Hogrefe, Russell, eds. *Group Work in Community Life.* New York: Association Press, 1954.

National Conference of Social Work. *Group Work and Community Organization, 1953–54.* New York: Columbia University Press, 1954.

———. *Selected Papers in Group Work and Community Organization.* Raleigh, N. C.: Health Publications Institute, 1951.

———. *Selected Papers in Group Work and Community Organization.* Raleigh, N. C.: Health Publications Institute, 1952.

Phillips, Helen U., ed. *Achievement of Responsible Behavior through Group Work Process.* Philadelphia: University of Pennsylvania School of Social Work, 1950.

Sullivan, Dorothea, ed. *Readings in Group Work.* New York: Association Press, 1952.

Trecker, Harleigh B. *Social Group Work: Principles and Practices* (revised edition). New York: Whiteside, Inc., 1955.

Trecker, Harleigh B., ed. *Group Work Foundations and Frontiers.* New York: Whiteside, Inc., and William Morrow & Company, 1955.

――――. *Group Work in the Psychiatric Setting.* Proceedings of an Institute conducted by the American Association of Group Workers, 1955. New York: Whiteside, Inc., and William Morrow & Company, 1956.

Wilson, Gertrude, and Ryland, Gladys. *Social Group Work Practice: the Creative Use of the Social Process.* Boston: Houghton Mifflin Company, 1949.

Wittenberg, Rudolph. *So You Want to Help People; a Mental Hygiene Primer for Group Leaders.* New York: Association Press, 1947.

――――. *The Art of Group Discipline; a Mental Hygiene Approach to Leadership.* New York: Association Press, 1951.

――――. *How to Help People; the Mental Hygiene Approach in Your Work with Youth.* New York: Association Press, 1953.

――――. *On Call for Youth: How to Understand and Help Young People.* New York: Association Press, 1955.

Unpublished Doctoral Dissertation

Northen, Helen. "The Effectiveness of Social Group Work in the Development of Qualitative Participation," 1953. (On microfilm at library of Bryn Mawr College, Bryn Mawr, Pa.)

Articles (Selected)

American Association of Group Workers Committee. "Definition of the Function of the Group Worker," *The Group,* XI, May, 1949. Reprinted in Harleigh B. Trecker, *Foundations and Frontiers.* New York: Whiteside, Inc., and William Morrow & Company, 1955.

Arcus, Sam George. "The Use of Time and Fee in the Intake Process of a Group Work Agency," *Jewish Social Service* Quarterly, XXVII, December, 1950; *Jewish Center Worker,* XII, January, 1951.

Bernstein, Daniel R. "Operation Street-Corner," *Journal of Social*

Work Process, VI. Philadelphia: Alumni Association and Faculty of the University of Pennsylvania School of Social Work, 1955.

Brager, George. "Group Autonomy and Agency Intake Practice," *Group Work and Community Organization, 1953–54.* Published for the National Conference of Social Work. New York: Columbia University Press, 1954.

Brueckner, William H. "The Group Worker's Commitment to Preparation of the Individual Toward Assuming Social Responsibilities," *Selected Papers in Group Work and Community Organization.* Published for the National Conference of Social Work. Raleigh, N. C.: Health Publications Institute, 1952.

Coyle, Grace L. "Group Work and Social Change," *Proceedings of the National Conference of Social Work,* XLII, 1935.

Festinger, Leon, and Coyle, Grace L. "Current Developments in Group Dynamics" and "The Relation of the Research Center for Group Dynamics to the Practice of Social Work," *Social Work in the Current Scene; Proceedings of the National Conference of Social Work,* LXXVII, 1950.

Jockel, Else, and Citron, Harry. "Promoting Social Recovery of State Hospital Patients Through the Group Process," *Journal of Social Work Process,* VII, 1956.

Kaiser, Clara A. "Group Work Education in the Last Decade," *The Group,* XV, June, 1953.

———. "Social Group Work Practice and Social Responsibility," *The Social Welfare Forum; Proceedings of the National Conference of Social Work,* LXXIX, 1952.

Kindelsperger, Walter L. "Employment Characteristics of the Recent Group Work Graduates, 1950–51–52," monograph. New York: National Social Welfare Assembly, 1953.

Middleman, Ruth R. "Arts and Crafts as a Group Centered Program," *The Group,* XVII, December, 1954.

Newstetter, Wilber I. "What Is Social Group Work?" *Proceedings of the National Conference of Social Work,* LXII, 1935.

Northen, Helen. "The Place of Agency Structure, Philosophy and Policy in Supporting Group Programs of Social Action," *The Group,* XI, Summer, 1949.

Osborn, Hazel, and Young, Harriet. "Some Factors of Resistance which Affect Group Participation," *The Group,* XI, January, 1949.

Phillips, Helen U. "Social Group Work—A Functional Approach," *The Group,* X, March, 1948.

————. "What Is Social Group Work Skill?" *The Group,* XVI, June, 1954.

Round Table, "The Group in Education, Group Work and Psychotherapy," *American Journal of Orthopsychiatry,* XXIV, January, 1954.

Scheidlinger, Saul. "Social Group Work and Group Psychotherapy," *Social Work,* I, July, 1956.

Seidler, Morris. "The Worker's Role in Social Action Programming with Youth Groups," in *Social Action Papers* presented at the Conference of the National Association of Jewish Center Workers, Atlantic City, June, 1950, *Jewish Center Worker* (Supplement), September, 1950.

Wilson, Gertrude. "Measurement and Evaluation of Social Group Work Practice," The Social Welfare Forum; *Proceedings of the National Conference of Social Work,* LXXIX, 1952.

SOCIAL SETTLEMENTS—SOURCES CITED

Addams, Jane. "Social Settlements," *Conference of Charities and Corrections,* XXIV, 1897.

Bosworth, Francis. "Settlements and Neighborhoods," *Social Work Year Book,* XII, 1954.

Elliott, John Lovejoy. "After 20 Years in the Tenement Houses of New York," address given before the Society for Ethical Culture, April, 1915; published in *The Standard,* I, 1915.

Hart, Helen. "The Changing Function of the Settlement under Changing Conditions," *Proceedings of the National Conference of Social Work,* LVIII, 1931.

Lathrop, Julia C. "Hull House as a Sociological Laboratory," *National Conference of Charities and Corrections,* XXI, 1894.

McDowell, John, et al. "Foreword and Statement of Purposes and Functions of Settlements in Cleveland," *Cleveland Settlement Study,* 1946.

Pacey, Lorene M., ed. *Readings in the Development of Settlement Work.* New York: Association Press, 1950.

Peabody, F. G. "Social Settlements," *Conference of Charities and Corrections,* XXIV, 1897.

Scudder, Vida D. "Settlement Past and Future," Denison House College Settlement Report, 1900; reprinted in Lorene M. Pacey, ed., *Readings in the Development of Settlement Work.* New York: Association Press, 1950.

"Symposium on Settlement Goals for the Next Third of a Century." Boston: National Federation of Settlements, 1926.

Vittum, Harriet E. "Politics from the Social Point of View," *Proceedings of the National Conference of Social Work*, LI, 1924.

Woods, Robert A. "The Settlement's Foothold of Opportunity," a communication sent to the First International Conference of Settlements at London, July, 1922; published in Robert A. Woods, *The Neighborhood in Nation-building*. Boston: Houghton Mifflin Company, 1923.

Woods, Robert A., and Kennedy, Albert J. *The Settlement Horizon*. New York: Russell Sage Foundation, 1922.

SOCIAL WORK REFERENCES CITED
(Other than Social Group Work)

Coyle, Grace L. "The Role of the Faculty Member in the Creation of an Integrated Program," unpublished paper presented at the 33rd annual meeting of the American Association of Schools of Social Work, New York, January, 1952.

Flexner, Abraham. "Is Social Work a Profession?" *Proceedings of the National Conference of Charities and Corrections*, XLII, 1915.

Leichter, Elsa. "Family Casework Through the Group Method," *Journal of Jewish Communal Service*, XXXII, Summer, 1956.

Peck, Harris B., and Bellsmith, Virginia. *Treatment of the Delinquent Adolescent; Group and Individual Therapy with Parent and Child*. New York: Family Service Association of America, 1954.

Pray, Kenneth L. M. *Social Work in a Revolutionary Age*. Philadelphia: University of Pennsylvania Press, 1949.

Rappaport, Mazie. "Casework with Adolescent, Delinquent Girls: the Dynamics of Expectation as a Psychological Concept in Working with Adolescent, Delinquent Girls," unpublished paper presented at the National Conference of Social Work, Atlantic City, April, 1948.

Robinson, Virginia P., ed. *Training for Skill in Social Case Work* (Social Work Process Series). Philadelphia: University of Pennsylvania Press, 1942.

Taft, Jessie. "The Relation of Function to Process in Social Case Work," *The Journal of Social Work Process*, I, 1937.

Wessel, Rosa, and Faith, Goldie Basch. *Professional Education*

Based in Practice. Philadelphia: University of Pennsylvania School of Social Work, 1953.

GENERAL REFERENCES CITED

Adler, Alfred. *Social Interest: a Challenge to Mankind.* London: Faber & Faber, Ltd., 1938; New York: G. P. Putnam's Sons, 1938.

Allee, Warder C. *Animal Aggregations.* Chicago: University of Chicago Press, 1931.

————. *The Social Life of Animals.* New York: W. W. Norton & Company, 1938.

Allen, Frederick H. *Psychotherapy with Children.* New York: W. W. Norton & Company, 1942.

Ashley-Montagu, M. F. *On Being Human.* New York: Henry Schuman, 1950.

————. *The Directions of Human Development.* New York: Harper & Brothers, 1955.

Cantor, Nathaniel. "Function and Focus in the Learning Process," *Journal of Educational Research,* XLV, November, 1951.

Cartwright, Dorwin, and Zander, Alvin, eds. *Group Dynamics, Research and Theory.* Evanston, Ill.: Row, Peterson & Company, 1953.

Cherbonnier, E. LaB. *Hardness of Heart.* Garden City, N. Y.: Doubleday & Company, 1955.

Cunningham, Ruth, and Associates. *Understanding Group Behavior of Boys and Girls.* New York: Teachers College, Columbia University, 1951.

de Mille, Agnes. *Dance to the Piper.* Boston: Little, Brown & Company (Atlantic Monthly Press book), 1952.

Dewey, John. *Art as Experience.* New York: G. P. Putnam's Sons, 1934.

Ghiselin, Brewster, ed. *The Creative Process, a Symposium.* Berkeley and Los Angeles: University of California Press, 1952.

Kluckhohn, Clyde, Murray, Henry A., and Schneider, David M. *Personality, Society and Culture,* 2nd ed. New York: Alfred A. Knopf, 1953.

Linton, Ralph, *The Tree of Culture.* New York: Alfred A. Knopf, 1955.

Mead, Margaret, and Wolfenstein, Martha, eds. *Childhood in Contemporary Cultures.* Chicago: University of Chicago Press, 1955.

Muller, Herbert J. *Science and Criticism.* New Haven: Yale University Press, 1943.

————. *The Uses of the Past*. New York: Oxford University Press, 1952.

Rank, Otto. *Will Therapy and Truth and Reality*. Translated with a preface and introduction by Jessie Taft. New York: Alfred A. Knopf, 1945.

Redl, Fritz, and Wineman, David. *Children Who Hate; the Disorganization and Breakdown of Behavior Controls*. Glencoe, Ill.: Free Press, 1951.

————. *Controls from Within; Techniques for the Treatment of the Aggressive Child*. Glencoe, Ill.: Free Press, 1952.

Sinnott, Edmund W. *Cell and Psyche: the Biology of Purpose*. Chapel Hill: University of North Carolina Press, 1950.

Taft, Jessie. "Living and Feeling," *Child Study*, X, January, 1933.

Whitehead, Alfred North. *The Aims of Education*. New York: The Macmillan Company, 1929.

————. *Science and the Modern World*. New York: The Macmillan Company, 1925.

UNPUBLISHED RECORDED MATERIAL USED

IN THIS PUBLICATION

I. On file at the University of Pennsylvania School of Social Work
   A. Advanced Curriculum Project
      Citron, Harry. "Learning to Value Choice in the Helping Process While Offering Groups of Chronic Patients in a State Mental Hospital an Opportunity to Discover and Test for Themselves Their Own Will Direction and the Strength of Their Impulse Toward New Life," 1955.
   B. Masters' Theses
      Bernstein, Daniel R. "Helping a Nine-Year-Old, Inarticulate Boy Use Group Experience to Find a Self He Can Share," 1950.
      Shapiro, Sidney. "The Present Experience as the Worker's Focus in Enabling a Group of Dependent Older Adult Men to Discover and Affirm a Belief in Their Capacity to Achieve," 1953.
   C. Student Papers (Untitled)
      Attinson, Zita—1952
      Bartram, T. Smedley—1950
      Beckerman, Aaron—1953
      Sternbach, Jacob—1955

II. On file at Social Agencies

    Shorefront Jewish Community Centers, Brooklyn, N. Y.
      Student-worker (New York University)—Herman Resnick
    Springfield Jewish Community Center, Springfield, Mass.
      Worker—Sidney Shapiro
    Wharton Centre, Philadelphia
      Worker—Daniel R. Bernstein